D1329385

Secret of
The Dormant
Brain Lab

Niles Abercrumby and
The Book of Wands

By Neil Slade

Illustrated by BRIAN GIES

Brain Books and Music

Denver, CO

Secret of The Dormant Brain Lab

Niles Abercrumby and The Book of Wands

Copyright 2011

All Rights Reserved

Neil Slade Books and Music

PO Box 6799, Denver, CO 80206

www.NeilSlade.com

www.TheBookOfWands.com

neil@neilslade.com

ISBN 978-0-9796363-3-2

Second Edition, March 2011

For Mom, Dad, and Karen
Chloe, Erfie, Molly, Tippy,
Tammy, Willo, Voncie,
Homer, and Quinn

Special thanks to Jim Mullica
for his contributions
and perspective
in the preparation of this edition.

And of course

T.D.A. Lingo

WARNING!!

This book should be kept out of the reach of children.

It is advised that adults in the possession of this book take precautions to keep it hidden in such places so not as to arouse interest in readers under the age of 18, and certainly in the case of potential readers under the age of 12 years of age.

Recommended areas of safe keeping include but are not limited to refrigerator vegetable compartments and laundry areas, as well as more obvious, hence unlikely spaces such as bookcases and library shelves. It is suggested that such hiding places be rotated for the most effective levels of security.

Exposure to vulnerable young children and adolescents may result in irreparable harm to conventional thinking, including a serious reduction in television viewing and/or video and computer game engagement.

If a child or other susceptible person is exposed to certain content contained within this volume it may lead to a dangerously expanded vocabulary as well as increased awareness and/or research of scientific, literary, and artistic references. It may result in an unwanted increase in attention span that may extend to as long as thirty minutes to one hour or more in one twenty-four hour period. It may also be found to propagate unwanted long term interest in reading itself or other activities indirectly referred to in this book such as strenuous physical exercise.

Such repercussions may require informed explanations of words and content, or worse yet, actual adult guidance and/or involvement in newly acquired interests or study which is to be avoided at all costs. In the case of accidental intellectual and creative curiosity aroused at any age, immediately consult a qualified specialist.

Please handle with care and take all necessary safety measures. The publishers are not responsible for any damage. Thank you.

Author's Note:
Secret of The Dormant Brain Lab
Niles Abercrumby and The Book of Wands

This series of memoirs is a recollection of some of the more notable events of my life from my youth to the present. Some of the names have been changed to protect the privacy of individuals as needed. With minor exceptions, the stories in this book accurately reflect true events.

Please also note that when a Wand or Unusual Tool is mentioned, as well as the process of using such (Travel), the word is capitalized to distinguish it from an ordinary object and its use, in keeping with the tradition.

This volume is the first of four parts of
The Book of Wands.

SPECIAL NOTE:
To access real photos and special illustrations from Niles Abercrumby and The Book of Wands go on the Internet to:

www.BookOfWands.com/treasure/secrets.html

User ID: secrets888
Password: tickleamygdala

Contents

THE

BOOK

OF

WANDS

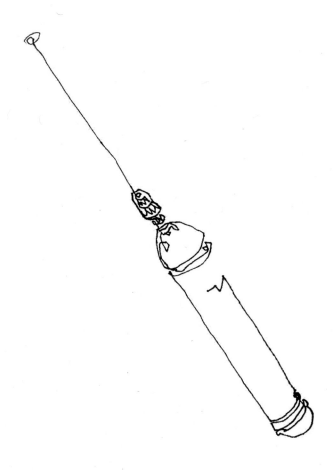

BOW WOW 1
Greetings

I am The Book of Wands.
Nice to meet you.
You might be expecting to be reading a book. Haha. ☺
This is different.

I show the Way of Wands, and this has inspired some to fondly refer to me and my method as BOW WOW.

A Paper Leaf Ensemble, thusly:
You know that you aren't the clothes that you are wearing. Similarly, these pages are also only just my clothes, what I am wearing at the moment. You are holding my socks.

What you see are letters printed on a page, symbols made up of microscopic smudges imprinted on bound sheets of flattened dried wood pulp, what people commonly refer to as a "book".

Indeed, however, I am in fact not a bunch of sentences, a few hundred paper pages that have been stitched together in the basement of a print shop, in a dusty old building, on the outskirts of a big city far away.

Rather, this is my portrait, a paint by number ink splat collection bound together, pages that are perhaps stapled together here, or loosely thrown in a box over there, or maybe even glued on a paper spine in another place.

Instead,
I am the originator.
Please focus beyond what you read to see ME.
Thank you.

I thought this thought which was then hammered out by someone's fingers on a clickity clack letter embossed checkerboard. Tappity tap tap tap dance duet of two hands into a code of reflected light and dark now shining upon your face.

I tickled someone's brain to excitedly wiggle his ten fingers over a Keyboard, and that produced this arrangement of marks that lightly scurry over your rods and cones like a team of untamed hamsters on ice skates.

Tickly tickle tickle. Scurry scurry scurry.

In the case of an audible incarnation of one form or another, a human speaking my words with their mouth and perhaps captured on a recording of some sort, I ride upon compressed air waves like a bronco buster upon a wild horse of crazy ideas. The steed gallops full bore out from the corral of vibrating vocal cords and dances around the rodeo ring of a vibrating paper cone inside a cheering speaker box. Ride 'em cowboy!

I continually twist and turn at the speed of light. I am an aural pixie, skipping across iridescent purple inorganic atoms, then shaking hands with glowing blue organic electrons at the entrance of a grinning neural network.

I enter your inner ear labyrinth, whirl around your cochlea whirlpool into your cranium like a super silly microbe on a lubricated water slide.

Zip zap zoop.

So then, this is Me transmitting direct to you through one code or another.

Helloooooooooo.

Still, to be clear, I am not the duplicated sound dancing on the internal high wire of a reader's throat, I'm not a celluloid record bound wiggle, nor the dancing trapeze wire signals inside a human's brain. Nor am I the printed lettuce and tomato in an ink sandwich between two hard covers.

I live outside any container, flesh, bone, wood, paper, metal, or otherwise.

Understand this, and you too will be set free.

See me as I truly am, and you will begin to Travel.
And to Travel, my good new friend, is to live.

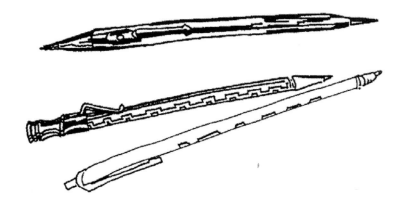

PART ONE:

SECRET OF
THE DORMANT
BRAIN LAB

Chapter 0
Prologue

We had driven up the Mt. Evanescence road riding in a sleek white mouse-sized vintage sports car. We pulled in next to a giant granite boulder that was perhaps ten or twelve feet high. The rock dwarfed the vehicle as one's hand might overshadow such a diminutive furry rodent.

We locked the car and took a good look around. Here we were at over twelve-thousand feet, stepping out onto the gravel, a small pullout, a minimalist parking lot, if you could call it that.

There was virtually nothing about but small alpine plants and stone as far as the eye could see. Much of it looked just like the Scottish Highlands, but that place was on the other side of the globe. The air was cool, and the sky- what parts of it that we could see through the clouds- was a perfect and flawless cobalt blue.

I had been to the place we would soon be hiking many times before, onto an area of the mountain that few tourists knew about or had bothered to explore. I had collected enough strange tales to fill a volume. I knew Bobby was in for an extraordinary experience. However, in no way could I predict exactly what that experience would be. The place was mystery personified.

Here above timberline we were very nearly completely removed from our every day life, detached from the energies and influences that effectively contaminate the consciousness of everyone who is in the middle of that madness we call "civilization".

Remarkably, we were barely an hour's drive from the metropolitan area that we lived in. Looking east we could see the sprawling city far below us through a thick humid haze as if we were looking down on earth from outer space, a gaseous cloud of cosmic vapor between us and the rest of the universe.

"This is amazing," my young student Bobby said. "This is like another world."

And we hadn't even walked away from the car yet.

I went around to the trunk and opened it. It creaked.

"Take a Wand," I said. "Do you want the Cane or the Umbrella?" I scratched my nose.

Bobby looked up. "Hmmm. Looks like it might rain. I'll take the Umbrella."

"Good choice," I said as I handed him the unusual and rare wangee handled tool. It was among my favorite Wands, and I was certain that he would pick up something good with it. The signals were exceptionally clear in that area and I was certain it would afford him access to information that he would never be able to get otherwise.

That the Umbrella might keep him dry if necessary was almost entirely beside the point.

I took the Chinese Sword Cane for myself. I was actually relieved, because frankly I didn't think he had enough experience to use it yet. He was still pretty green and he might end up putting a hole in his foot or worse, even though the sword was for the moment safely sheathed inside the hollow barrel of the Cane.

The whole purpose of our expedition was to cement in Bobby's mind the experience for himself- that he was surrounded by Unusual Tools, tools that everyone else took for granted as being nothing special at all.

It was my hope that he would at last see that these very tools could open up doors for him, that these tools could launch him far from his common experience into other worlds that otherwise seemed only a dream. It was my hope that the two Wands we had brought with us high into the mountains would reveal their potential in a manner that he could no longer deny as nothing more than my fertile imagination.

Nearly everyone else on the planet thought that the idea of Wands was just make-believe. Nearly everyone else on the planet thought I was out of my mind when I brought up the topic- an increasingly rare event. (Until now, my dear reader. Not unusual that people think that I am out of my mind- but rare that I've broached the topic in public.)

We removed our packs from the back of the car and I shut the trunk.

"You know, I once locked my keys in the car out here seconds after my friend told me not to. It took us about five hours to get to the nearest town and find a locksmith." I held up my keys in my hand. "Won't do that again."

"Why don't you get one of those magnetic key holder things?" Bobby asked.

"This," I paused dramatically, "Is a plastic car." I patted the fender affectionately.

I had driven us up in my little bitty white 1965 Lotus Elan. This was a very rare and very tiny fiberglass sports car, a one-hundred and twenty mile per hour streamlined go-cart that made any sleek Chevy Corvette or Ferrari look absolutely obese. The little British urban racer ate up Colorado mountain roads like an effortless quick snack between breakfast and brunch.

Years before, in a colossal demonstration of being in just the right place at the right time, I had managed to acquire the car with not much more money than a family might spend on a few days vacation at Disneyworld. I had wanted one of these since I had been fourteen years old, but anymore, they were impossible to come by. For me, the car was a testament to the power of real magic in transporting one to one's dream world.

I pulled on my backpack and began to walk on an almost imperceptible dirt trail. The faint path wound away from the car park towards the backbone of a peak that lay in the short distance in front of us.

"Follow me, the best is just ahead. You haven't seen anything yet," I enthusiastically predicted.

Sure enough, a moment later, "*ACK!!*" Something gnarly had painfully caught my foot and not six feet from the car I stubbed my toe on a sharp rock that was jutting out from the trail. I barely kept my balance.

"Ooo, *ouch!!*" I stopped and rubbed my toe, grimacing and wobbling on the on the un-stubbed leg.

"Hahah!" Bobby laughed. "Oh man, how long have you been giving these guided tours? Hahahha!... *OWWUUPP!!!*"

Bobby was so busy laughing at me that he had stumbled on the very same rock himself. He did a jumbled and twisted clown-ballet pirouette, and then fell flat with a big thump on his rear end.

I smiled broadly with a decidedly self-satisfied grin, "Ha. Ha. Ha." My sore foot completely stopped hurting.

"Shuddup…" he said, embarrassed. He pushed himself up and dusted off his pants.

"People who live in housed glasses shouldn't stow thrones," I commented.

"What?" Bobby questioned with a furrowed brow as he picked several small pieces of imbedded gravel out from his palms.

"Forget it," I smiled. "You okay?"

"Yes, thank you very much."

I was more than three times the age of my young teenage guitar student, my Traveling protégé on that day. Unlike myself, he had never made the excursion before, to that unique high altitude paradise.

I knew the landscape as well as I knew my own urban back yard. But the place still retained its secrets from me, even in the many spots that I was intimately familiar with. I never tired of exploring every nook and cranny up on that mountain, and there seemed to be an endless supply of both.

On brief reflection, however, I must honestly admit I actually have no idea what a cranny is or what might distinguish it from a nook.

We had driven a few miles up the long winding road that peeled off from the main two-laned highway now a long distance below. There was no sound at all.

We had not seen another single vehicle of any type. Although the road commonly had cars traveling the majestic scenic lane during any summer weekend, I had purposefully chosen a weekday for this trip to avoid exactly that. I wanted the mountain to ourselves.

We certainly would not run into anyone off the road and to where we were headed, onto the edge of a long line of rocky cliffs. We might see a pica or a crow, but I expected few other moving creatures save a bug here or there.

We had now walked several hundred yards from the car and quite a vertical distance in elevation higher up. Our vehicle now looked like a matchbox sized toy car far below us.

We zig-zagged the most crooked indirect path winding higher and higher, in between the boulders ever increasing in size. The wildflowers surrounded us, and were at their most colorful and splendid peak.

"Look at this!" Bobby exclaimed with surprise, his sudden dramatic outburst taking me by surprise as well. "These flowers, this is incredible! They're huge, they're absolutely huge!"

I turned around and looked at him as he held aloft a tiny blossom. I was puzzled and didn't understand what he meant. They were just regular little wildflowers. "Huge?... Huh?" I queried.

Bobby held up a picked purple stem right in front of his one opened eye, looking back down at the Lotus far below. "Niles, look! This flower is actually bigger than your car!"

It took a second, but I then smiled and understood the joke. "Hey! You're not supposed to pick the flowers up here. It's a nature reserve." I frowned slightly and shook my head in disapproval.

"Oh, sorry." Bobby knelt down and made an utterly ridiculous attempt to replant the flower back in the ground. He was mocking me, in a good natured way as was his habit. His pantomime was actually absurdly funny.

"Forget it. Just don't pick any more. If everybody who came up here picked one flower every day for the next ten-thousand years, pretty soon there wouldn't be any left," I lectured.

"Ha." Bobby said. "Funny."

However, the reality *was* that it actually was prohibited to pick anything up in this wilderness. Tourists had already created significant damage to the ancient forest that lay a half a mile downhill from where we hiked.

Mt. Evanescence was home to some of the oldest trees on the entire planet- bristlecone pines, the oldest living things on earth. We walked a mere quarter-mile above them and could see the ghostly odd angled dark branches of the enchanted forest peeking through the ground fog below us. Any moment I expected to see goblins run out from behind one of the nearby truck sized boulders we passed and dash off into the dark woods below.

Before the area was protected by law, and surely even afterward, tourists had regularly picked up and taken away gorgeous pieces of ancient dead wood that was an irreplaceable part of the natural environment. Close to the road itself where people drove to access this area, the ground was nearly as bare as a beach.

But up where we were hiking the story was different. We were above tree line itself, which we could see as a distinct border several hundred feet below us. Where the forest came up the hill nearer to where we were, far from the road, it was too far for lazy flat-landers to venture. This end of the enchanted forest remained pristine and whole, unspoiled- and unpicked.

There was an incredible abundance of wild flowers everywhere. There were Purple Sparklers that looked like violet fireworks shooting off a green rocket trail with gold bursts in the center of each brilliant blossom. There were snow stars hugging the ground, no more than a quarter inch across each, as delicate as fairy footprints. There were football field sized patches of Indian

Paintbrush here and there in an infinite variety of subtle shades of ruby, scarlet, orange, and yellow. And then there were the Giant Pluto Heads, big green round balls of spikes that truly looked like they belonged at the bottom of an extraterrestrial ocean.

It was impossible not to stare at our feet as we climbed higher and higher towards the crest of the peak in front of us. The ground was an unbelievably psychedelic and detailed landscape of multi-colored pebbles, plants, and moss, and it was hard to keep your eyes off of it.

Bobby came up behind me and tapped me on the shoulder. "This is like being... um, gee... I don't know..." he remarked. "All I had for lunch was peanut butter..."

I smiled, but didn't say anything. I knew exactly what he was talking about.

In the city, you would not think twice about such patterns under your feet. You would think such simple things as small plants and stones were entirely unremarkable. But in that rarified environment, something instantly clicked inside your brain. You became super sensitive to subtle variations of texture and color that struck you as entirely magnificent. The effect might be compared to taking a powerful shamanic concoction, but the potion was that special place itself.

We began to reach the top of one crest and had long lost sight of the car. As we rounded a small outcropping of rock, we stopped and took in a view that was nothing short of breathtaking, literally.

"Hold on a minute," Bobby said. "I'm outta' breath!" He bent down with his hands on his knees.

"Wimp," I boasted. "I'm a Capricorn. What are you, Pisces the trout?"

"Hey. I'm a Capricorn too. I'm just not used to this."

"Too much pasta." I retorted. I figure his name wasn't Bobby Spaghetti for nothing.

"You're suppose to carb up when you go on a hike, don't you know?" Bobby replied.

I chucked to myself. Here was a young teenager, and he was having trouble keeping up with me, an old fart. Of course, I didn't dare mention that my thighs were already aching from the steep leg of the trail we had just come up. I was actually glad he wanted to rest.

"Look at that," I pointed out the range of snowcapped peaks immediately across the valley to the west.

Bobby straightened up and turned around to look. "Oh wow," he said nearly under his breath. "That's incredible."

We were looking at not one, but several fourteen-thousand foot peaks all within eyeshot from that vantage point. The very summit of Mt. Evanescence was just mere miles from where we stood. Gray and Torries twin fourteeners were a short distance west. Long's Peak was up-range perhaps twenty-five miles. Pike's Peak was a relatively far fifty miles south of where we stood. But we could see them all within an easy turn of our heads.

"Let's keep going, there's a vector window just over there," I suggested and pointed a short distance away. Bobby looked puzzled. "Um, a very interesting place," I clarified.

We hiked down a bit, hopping from the top of one flat boulder to the next, but still staying more or less on the crest of the rocky expanse we were exploring. To our immediate right eastward, the hillside dropped sharply, forming a wall of granite bluffs that ended two-hundred feet below us at the edge of the bristlecones. To our left, the side of the mountain more gradually descended into a long deep valley. We made our way along the west side of the ridge, continually working our way higher and higher.

After another ten minutes of hiking up and down a rocky roller coaster we came to an unexpectedly wide flat area that was oddly private and enclosed, right in the middle of an area that was for the most part completely exposed to the elements otherwise.

"This is it," I said as I took off my back pack and sat down on the ground to get out a drinking bottle. "You want some?"

I handed Bobby the water bottle after taking a good long swig myself.

"Shortstop," he said.

I smiled. I had heard my father use that expression when I was a kid and used the salt before passing it on. My father's spirit must have been following us that afternoon.

Bobby walked over to a high solid wall of rock that sat on one side of the flat area. It was as if we had suddenly stumbled upon a big outdoor movie screen that had been carved out of the side of the mountain.

"I didn't expect to see any of this," he said as he ran his hand against the wall. For Bobby, it all must have been quite something to encounter for the first time. "This is awesome," he said surveying the landscape. I forgave the cliché.

There was also a small ledge about three feet off the ground at the base of the wall. I watched as Bobby contemplated the spot with his back towards me. He threw his own backpack and the Umbrella on the ground. Then he placed one foot on the ledge testing it for his weight.

It was as if instinct took over and he dug his fingernails into the rock face and then hoisted himself wholly onto the lip. He flattened himself against the wall, hugging it, his ear to the wall as if he was listening to something deep inside the earth.

Looking at him flat against the rock cliff, it made the most incongruous sight. Here he was standing vertically against this nearly perfectly flat area, a wall perhaps twenty-five feet across and twenty feet high, and yet from my vantage point it looked exactly as if he were lying down on a granite bed horizontally. It was a remarkable illusion.

He closed his eyes.

There was no sound at all; no wind, no birds, no nothing.

And then we heard in the distance, from the direction of the twisted fifteen-hundred year old pine trees below us, a sound as sudden as a crack of thunder piercing the clouds high above us, a sound that sent a bolt of pure electrical shock up our spines.

Bobby was catapulted off the wall no different than if the wall itself had suddenly come to life and knocked him off with the force of a heavy weight boxer. But it wasn't the clouds bashing each other above our heads that we had heard.

We had both heard the unmistakable sustained sound of someone screaming at the top of their lungs from within the forest below, as if they were seconds away from being murdered.

"Get up!!" I yelled as I jumped to my feet, my Cane in my hand held out at arm length." Grab your Wand! Now!!"

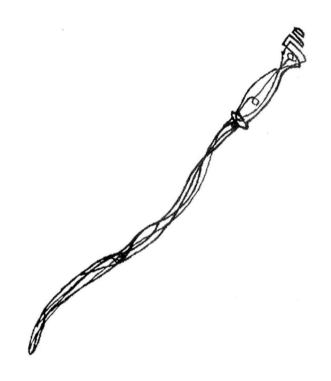

Chapter 1
Niles Abercrumby

I met Frank Zappa one Denver summer night in 1973. My high school buddy Scott Limburger and I had snuck into the KFML FM radio station building where Frank was giving an interview before the show.

He had been my hero for years. I worshipped him as a composer and a cultural rebel.

We first peered at him through the glass studio window inside, and then accosted him on his way out. I will always remember the very first words that he had spoken to me. He said, "Wait a minute, I have to go to the bathroom."

When he returned, Frank was polite and cordial. He gave me one single bit of advice, along with his ball point pen autograph on the outside of a crinkled used envelope that I had stuffed into my pocket, the only scrap of paper I had at hand at the moment:

"Remember you are employed, and working for the muse."

My name is Niles Abercrumby.

I've taught over thirty-thousand music lessons in my life to an uncounted number of pupils, with a few students thrown in. Very few.

I've taught an even select fewer of those to use Wands.

I am a university trained musician with a teaching certificate in Music Education from the state of Colorado, United States of America, Earth, Solar System, Milky Way Galaxy, Universe 14RCB Sector 42, Reality Phase 9. I earned this certificate many, many years ago.

I've long outgrown it, and I let it expire and die of natural causes five short years after it arrived in my mail box. It came in a big white envelope packed along with my diploma as well as an application for car insurance.

My teaching certificate and college diploma were mailed to me since I had not received such documents ceremoniously in person with a handshake and wearing the traditional cap and gown. Nor had I less ceremoniously obtained it either, as conceivably wearing mere plain jeans and sneakers with holes in each, the certificate slid through the opening of a bullet proof teller window inside the administration office building by a smiling cherubic clerk with a Hispanic surname.

I opted for the much more informal U.S. Postal Mail delivery option. Less walking for me, same end result without all the pomp and pageantry. I'm not big on ceremony.

In college I learned how to play every band instrument that John Phillips Sousa wrote an arrangement for. I also as learned how to toot and pluck on every instrument used in a modern day symphonic orchestra, those instruments that I already had not taught myself to play out of curiosity growing up. I was always very interested in music and doing things with my hands, but I was never interested in institutions or tradition per se.

It is no coincidence that the same dexterity applied to instruments helps in the channeling of energy through an assortment of Unusual Tools. However, there is presently no college course on the proper employment of such tools, nor is there any diploma associated with this skill. I earned my extra-curricular skill without documentation or accreditation. I learned the How-To of Wands directly from studying the only real source of literature I know of on the subject, and from trial and error.

As I've come to learn, Wand technique greatly relies on the underlying Fun-da-Mental principals that I learned from the one person who was responsible for allowing me to get my hands on a copy of such a textbook on the subject. This person, almost certainly a Wand practitioner himself during his life, was considered by the general public as wildly eccentric at the very least, if not outright out of his mind.

Indeed, my first direct knowledge of Unusual Tools and how they work came as a result of spending an awful lot of time with a fellow that most people thought was just some crazy old guy living in a shack up in the mountains.

High up in a remote forest near the Colorado Continental Divide lived and worked the founder and director of The Dormant Brain Research and Development Laboratory, D.A.T. Stingo, or as we called him, DaStingo, or even simpler, Stingo.

I've always found that a person's name reveals something about their character, and this seems to be the case with everyone that's played a significant role in this story.

In his case, Stingo was a tough professor and teacher. He didn't mess around. He could give you the most powerful injection of truth and wisdom of anyone I had ever met as well as a huge shot of inspiration and energy. But he also had a sharp bite if you made the fatal mistake of taking him for a fool. You could get stung badly, and you wouldn't forget.

Up until now, his involvement with Wands has remained a complete secret to nearly every one of the students and subjects who passed through the stone gate to his pristine wilderness facility.

In all respects it was already a place off the most un-beaten track. For him to further admit to utilizing Wands would have pushed his already teetering reputation even further off center and completely off the precipice of doubtful acceptance.

Had Stingo revealed his interest and knowledge, much less professed a use of Wands, he would have certainly been considered a complete lunatic by all, including his most ardent supporters. Thus, it went unadvertised to his grave.

The main work of Stingo's behavior lab was teaching people the ins and outs of how their mind motor worked, learned in the atmosphere of nature unspoiled.

You see, Stingo wanted to save the world, one person at a time.

He felt that the world was a mess because most people had a mess of a brain. Multiply a messy brain by billions of brain owners, and you get a messy and doomed planet.

If you can save *one* brain, that brain can save another. "Each one, teach one," he would say. And with that, a geometric progression would begin. "Save one soul, and you save the universe," an ancient script echoed from the past.

My self-imposed job was to see if I could save myself for a start.

If you managed to hear about and to actually find The Dormant Brain Lab and its director-caretaker, you might sign up for a six-week Brain In Nature Course. You would camp out for weeks on end, sleep on hard stone covered ground in your self-made lean-to shelter, and at the end of the summer you would have enough knowledge of how the human brain works to teach a university crash course on the subject.

Then you would go home.

To all of the hundreds of people who found their way to that back woods institute and completed the course, brain training would remain their only impression of what Stingo and his place was all about.

But quite out of view, hidden far off the main trail proper was a key to tools that would surely land anyone locked admission into the funny farm if they dared speak of it in public. It was here where I first learned of *The Book of Wands*.

Surely, no other former participants at the brain lab will confirm what I am about to reveal, mainly because they just weren't in on this most secretive of Stingo's secrets. They all split once they got from him what they wanted and what they expected to get.

"Once a student pops his frontal lobes," Stingo often remarked, "I never see 'em again."

I hung around years after everyone else had gone home to feed their goldfish. As it turned out, something else turned up on the end of my line.

During his life Stingo did not want to jeopardize the rest of his work and his already counter-culture reputation by even wilder claims now set forth in my own account here. I can afford such a personal risk as I already have a steady and permanent income selling thousands of battery operated pet nail trimmers on eBay each month under a completely different name.

So let us proceed.

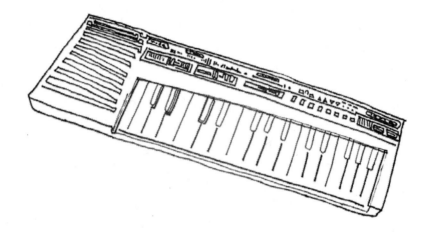

Chapter 2
The Niles Abercrumby
School of Music
And Other Stuff

My Wand exposure and education began as early as I can remember, although I didn't realize nor was I told that I was obtaining such instruction indirectly or otherwise until far later on.

My grandma gave me my first Wand for my sixth birthday. It came attached to a long playing phonograph record entitled *Conduct Your Own Orchestra*. It was a long black plastic Baton, and the idea was that as you listened to orchestral favorites on the record player you would wave your Baton along with the music. This was rudimentary Travel in that I was actually glimpsing my own true future.

In fact, before I was twenty-one years of age, I was leading an orchestra- at least in conducting class at the university. Additionally, I would lead numerous other musical ensembles throughout my life. I rather doubt if any other user of that album and the Wand that came with it actually shared a similar fortune.

Of course, the record absolutely did not advertise the stick as a Wand for Travel, but rather supplied the would-be conductor with more regular expectations and directions for use.

Using a Wand as a Wand is almost universally unadvertised as such. Understandably, claims one would make of such an activity would lead others to the perception that one has lost all his marbles. But I diverge.

I refused to go to my university graduation, held early one summer Saturday morning, because I felt that achieving my higher education had already robbed me enough of my own personal time. I had already missed hundreds of hours of early weekend Bugs Bunny cartoons during my youth because of Saturday morning religious school that my parents forced me to attend. Enough was enough already.

Speaking of religious school, I have never been particularly interested in religion either, with the possible exception of Taoism. That is clearly a pretty feeble excuse for an institutional belief system, but about as close to religion as I will ever voluntarily wander.

You know what those Taoists say: "The Way is not hard for those who have no preferences."

Well now, that's what I call religion.

When I graduated from college I immediately took a position as a substitute music teacher in the Denver Public Schools. That lasted for exactly one semester before I completely dropped out of classroom teaching. I had begun drinking a half gallon of coffee a day just to stay awake in class from the lack of creative stimulation inside my own head. I drank other potions to calm me down both on the way home and additionally after arriving home. My nerves were ritually being fried by junior high schoolers bouncing off the walls inside the hallowed and revered walled institution known as School.

Being that necessity is the mother of invention (and more on those Mothers later), and that my own survival seemed very necessary to me, I soon learned that I could make a perfectly comfortable living by inventing my own school, teaching music one person at a time at in-home private music lessons.

Thus, The Niles Abercrumby School of Music, Art and Other Stuff helped me to dodge brain atrophy and/or putting my nervous system at possible fatal risk from over-exposure to large numbers of wildly enthusiastic elementary, middle, and high school pupils.

Not that such public school classrooms are filled so much with students wildly enthusiastic about music, but more accurately are typically filled with pupils enthusiastic about being wild.

Speaking of students and pupils, one thing I do remember from my own middle school training, or at very least I continue to hallucinate, is that the difference between a pupil and a student is that a student studies, and a pupil simply watches.

It is easy to remember the differences between these two if you remember that a pupil is nothing but a hole that sucks in light.

The same classroom may be filled with thirty or more pairs of pupils, but may easily and simultaneously have zero students in it.

As I've said, necessity is the mother of invention, and so for me, it was necessary to make a living with music without losing my mind. I do however continue to be accused of already having met that fate. So it goes.

Speaking of mother, when I was in the sixth grade I earned my first few fistful of dollars self-employed, walking door to door in my neighborhood selling my own original pastel sketches. This was indeed chalk Wands at work making dollars in this most innocent manner.

I shocked my mother, herself a school teacher, when she found out how I had spent my afternoon mixing adolescent capitalism with crayons.

My mother is now 86, and she still can't believe, nor does she entirely approve of the idea that I actually make my living as a self-employed artist of any type.

Like I said, I let my teaching certificate expire because I never again wanted to voluntarily or otherwise set foot in a band room after an indoor winter and spring spent trying to wrestle order out of hundreds of entropy intent adolescent and younger bi-pedal hominids wielding drums, cymbals, horns, loud reed instruments, catgut strung boxes, and other "civilized" instruments of cacophony.

I continue to get my car insurance through my college, however, so my college education was not entirely wasted.

My mother had tried her best to sculpt me in her own image as a dedicated public school servant, but it was ultimately an exercise in futility for her part. My heart had been guided by another "Mother" throughout my teenage years:

I had grown up listening to the decadent and rebellious strains of Frank Zappa and The Mothers of Invention, as well as giving equal time listening and studying Captain Beefheart and His Magic Band. These were Dadaists with a tune.

Years after I had fled the public schools, Mom had still tried to convince me to keep my school teaching certificate valid. "You'll never know when you'll want to teach in the schools again!" she told me over and over.

I temporarily succumbed, and as I sat in the Colorado Teaching Certificate Renewal Study Seminar held at the Stapleton Airport Sheridan Hotel Conference Center, my mind kept drifting back to strains of Zappa compositions such as, "Who Are The Brain Police?" and "You're Probably Wondering Why I'm Here".

At the lunch break, sitting in a large cafeteria with a hundred or so soon to be re-certified re-fried public servants, I pondered my future in a just-emptied vanilla pudding cup that was part of our collective lunch break. I wondered how many more pudding cups I would stare blankly into in how many more noisy lunchroom cafeterias in the years to come. I took a quick deep breath and silently made a break for my car out in the parking lot, forever away from re-certification as if I were escaping from the penitentiary and a life sentence. I never looked back.

My resourcefulness in creating a career for myself as a private music teacher has had many distinct advantages over being employed by the state, not the least of which is that I get to stay home all day long and spend quality time with my dogs Erfie and Chloe, and practice with my Sticks, Wands, and other useful tools of Travel.

Erfie and Chloe are sleeping next to me on the couch right now as I write this

Yes indeed, you are now ingesting the thoughts of a person who while transcribing this at his particular longitude, latitude, and other dimensions and coordinates of time, space, and abstract thought, is sitting on a comfy three-cushioned sofa with semi-abstract southwestern Native American inspired geometrical designs imprinted on the fabric. Self-determination also allows this person to type at his own whim, day or night, with nary a care of waking up in time to join the mad rat race at seven A.M.

Next to him are two snoring and dreaming twin sibling West Highland White Terriers, each in their own, or perhaps other intersecting dog dreamy universes. They never dropped out of the rat race because they never joined it to begin with.

They have, contrary wise, chased smaller rodents across the kitchen floor. Fortunately my home has largely been rat free, albeit not free of their smaller and cuter cousins.

I hesitate to inform my companions that they have never actually caught a single mouse in their lives.

Wait!

I take that back.

One of them had actually deposited a big fat gray mouse at the foot of my bed a couple of months ago. That's probably why this particular rodent got caught in the first place- too chubby to run away fast enough.

Anyway, Erfie is the big brother, Chloe the little sister.

As I engage in interspecies telecommunication, tickling my amygdala forward and my frontal lobes on, I perceive the internal and non-corporal activities inside these somewhat smaller canine craniums:

Erfie, dreaming of a giant bowl, a white ceramic bowl decorated with colorful yellow flowers and blueberry and strawberry designs. It overflows with endless crunchy peanut butter and molasses dog biscuits.

Crunch crunch crunch.

Chloe, running through a wonderfully green hilly meadow, sun shining, birds twerping, butterflies dancing, clouds drifting, dandelion puffs riding on the wind. She runs to the top of the hill, wagging her tail- and at the top of a hill she comes upon a giant bowl of endless crunchy peanut butter and molasses doggy cookies.

Crunch crunch crunch.

I have no doubt at all who is the more intelligent of creatures, between humans and canines.

Despite the greater relative volume of the human brain, I humbly bow at the simple wisdom and generosity of my furry family members. Less is far more.

Chapter 3.1415926
The First Jar

You wouldn't know it by looking, but months and months have gone by since I last tap danced my fingers on my laptop Keyboard from two pages ago with the intention of notating this written history for any such person as yourself to eavesdrop upon.

Of course, YOU, my attentive listener, are indeed there. If a tree falls over in the forest and no squirrel or worm is there to hear it- (Does a worm have ears anyway?)- It does *not* in fact make a noise. Naturally, the converse is also true: If you weren't there to comprehend my descriptions then, well... then... um... of course you are, because you are... gosh, I am getting lost myself ... Hmmm. Okay, then... Uh...

Anyway, I have been putting most of this off for nearly a year now, but I can no longer delay the inevitable. Like Chloe barking and scratching at the back door wanting to come inside, the need for this written record has been making its presence ever more intense as each week passes.

Certainly, you must know what I mean. You've woken up early in the morning, perhaps only half out of a dream, hearing *that* persistent voice when you are in bed, still in your wrinkled and sweaty pajamas, and there is no place left to run away to. Your own conscience is staring at you from inside your skull and in no uncertain terms laying down the law. There is not enough room under your bed to hide away to. You know what lies ahead for you in the upcoming daylight. You cannot pull the covers up over your head any further than you already have.

In my case, I no longer have any doubt at all that my unfinished task must be completed, and that it is now more than ever immediately at hand. It is certain that I will be Traveling a great distance this time, and from all indications my farthest distance yet in one fell swoop.

For one aspect of this journey that I will share with you in this account, a tool that I will come to rely on, using it in the most ordinary fashion, my Wand used for typing here is of the complex variety, a portable alphabetic Keyboard.

Scoffed upon by purists, the portable Keyboard is a very distant cousin to simple Wands such as Pencils and Brushes. Of course it is an even more distant relative to the archetypal and classic mythical tool, the one that non-practitioners always think of when you mention the word *magic*, what is properly called a Baton. Commonly referred to as a "Wand" in the fictional literature, you know, Merlin waves his magic stick, hocus pocus presto chango- that is a Baton. They work, but not in that fairy tale fashion. You may shoo away a couple of mosquitoes by waving your Baton around, but Traveling with it takes a bit more finesse than that.

Besides that, truly learn Wands, and you realize that Wand Batons barely scratch the surface.

As for Keyboards, these are in another sub-category altogether, belonging to complex tools such as mechanical Pencils and spring loaded ballpoint Pens. And even then, Keyboards have branched off into their own sub-sub category onto a remote limb of the Unusual Tools tree and a very long stretch of evolution.

Some practitioners continue to vehemently deny the inclusion of any kind of Keyboard into the family of Extendio Humerous. E.H. of course refers to Unusual Tools that you utilize with an extended forearm. Obviously unlike most other Wands, a Keyboard does not resemble a stick or pole of any type. But neither do Cameras, Pendulums, Watches, or Cards, and those tools have long garnered fair inclusion into this family of unusual implements.

The fact is that you use a portable Keyboard with a relatively extended arm, although usually not completely straight as a baseball bat, but away from your body like any other Wand.

Naturally, Keyboard usage can produce the most mundane and ordinary results, like typing a letter or sending an email. But undeniably, in the hands of a trained and experienced master, like any other Wand you can use a decent Keyboard to more or less figuratively Travel to the sun and back- or for that matter, only hop around the block if that's all that you desire.

The idea of using a manual Typewriter as a Wand originally caused incredible disbelief and protest among seasoned Travelers. That lasted until word finally got around that one didn't pick up a Typewriter and wave it around like a Baton or blow on it like a clarinet, as many unsuccessfully tried to do.

Manual Typewriters finally caught on and things quieted down at last, at least for a while. This is similar to the kind of resistance that "The Earth Is Not Flat" idea initially met.

Then of course, came electric Typewriters. I'm still not so sure of those myself, because any time you are plugged into the wall there are issues. It restricts your movement severely. You can trip and hurt your ankle. You can unplug yourself if you're not careful and then everything will certainly and immediately grind to a sudden and disturbing halt. You may find yourself stuck face to face with a walking catfish on some swampy beach and without an exit.

Personally, I've never had much luck with cords. Generally, I avoid corded appliances altogether, except for my electric Guitars. You won't even find a blender in my house- not that a blender could ever conceivably qualify as a Wand. Haha. That's stupid.

Now of course, some Travelers are moaning about laptop computer Keyboards, and you would think it was the end of the world. Sure, trying to use a desktop computer as a Wand, that's ridiculous. Even if you could wave it around, you are sure to sprain something. But with even a cheap laptop Keyboard, there is no denying that you can get truly hard core Traveling done if you know how to handle it.

Of course, regarding Keyboards, some people who know absolutely nothing about Travel will completely get the wrong idea and think that the WORDS you hammer out with a Keyboard allow you to "Travel with your imagination". Oh gosh, how absurd. I can only imagine an adult would think of that one.

If you have actually Traveled somewhere, you don't have to imagine anything. You see it all with your own real eyeballs.

And then of course there are those portable musical Keyboards. They work too, but that's something altogether different. Alphabetic Keyboards are one thing, and Sonic Keyboards are another entirely.

My first real inkling of a Keyboard serving as a Wand of course came directly from the person who was both a Traveler and my brain teacher. I saw him using his Typewriter constantly, but it was years before he ever let on even slightly what he was really doing with the thing when nobody was watching. It wasn't until after he died that it hit me like the proverbial bolt from the blue what he was actually up to. But that is a story I will put off for just a short time, or at least until you turn enough pages.

So, ANYWAY,

Here we are.

You are my passenger. My electronic Pen is in my hand, my vehicle Key, my spaceship launch code. Buckle up. Do not leave your seat until the No Smoking sign vaporizes.

I have general ideas about my destination, and such coarse images are my inspiration and fuel. I will leave the delectable details to remain as a pleasant adventure and surprise, for this is both desirable and unavoidable as on any journey.

Where this will all lead, I surely have no exact and complete idea, although I am certain everything will be quite different, or at least as different as peach jam is different from chocolate sardines. Here we go now- leaving the land of smelly fish to land upon more fragrant shores.

But, Hurray! My own boredom with things as they are has set in, and escape is a great motivator. The silver lining of misery is the encouragement of change.

Time to move on and make a quantum leap off these pages. We will Travel together, myself and whoever hitchhikes along. That looks like you at the moment.

*   *   *

I was all set to live the perfect life. Or, as a cocky independent twenty-seven year old, so I thought so, keeping my deepest fears under wraps.

I was then living on my own in a little claustrophobic apartment in a rectangular brick six-unit building smack dab in the middle of Denver, Colorado. My apartment was one of hundreds of square, non-descript buildings located on an endless urban criss-cross grid of streets that had about as much personality as a screen door screen.

But then my life, at least on the surface, was less generic than most. Handsome (in my opinion), confident, healthy, I was additionally self-employed and running my own small stable of willing piano and guitar students. (Really, my ex-girlfriend had said I was indeed very handsome. That is before she broke up with me for being too short.)

When I dropped out of teaching in the public schools and first attempted being my own boss via the NASOMAOS (The Niles Abercrumby School of Music, Art, and Other Stuff), it didn't take very long to accumulate enough kid music students to make my rent and vegetarian hot dog buns each month.

Within fourteen days of getting my first two regularly paying students, I had sixteen more steady customers clamoring to have lessons every week. Word got around the neighborhood pretty fast that here was an opportunity to entertain the kids that wouldn't require even more schlepping them around after school.

Like wildfire, news spread that there was this fellow (me) who would come and teach junior and missy at-home music lessons right in the convenience of one's own basement wreck-room every week, and mom could watch her afternoon soaps completely uninterrupted, or whatever it is moms do after school.

But in spite of my modest early business success, things were really not going as smooth as banana cream pie despite the pretensions dictated by my young male ego. In reality, my future outlook and my self-assurance was as thin skinned as same banana, pre-piefied.

For one, despite my best efforts, I had made a habit of striking out in the romance department. My latest love disaster was with Sarah Jogurt, a more than lovely graduate of Vassar whom I had met at yoga class. She made her living making gorgeous white porcelain functional pottery. Alas, before long, her potter's studio trash can of discarded broken cups and saucers was soon joined by the fragments of my broken heart.

Of course for any young person, sheer hormone level in the blood stream dictate that one's love life sits high on the pedestal of positive self-esteem.

Unfortunately, the tonality of amore for Niles had been set long before. For starters, as early as in the sixth grade, with knees shaking I had one day miraculously managed to gather up enough courage to phone the object of my unrequited desire at the time, little cute elfin Cassie Boggs. She sat dolefully two rows over from me every day in Mr. Watson's home room class. I figured my chances with her were ripe for the plucking.

Age 12 years old, I picked up our kitchen's demure Princess model wall phone, paused for a moment, took a breath, and dialed.

"Hello…?", she answered.

"Hello, Cassie?"

"Yes."

"Um…uh… this is Niles."

"Niles?"

"Niles Abercrumby."

"Oh. *That* Niles."

My mother walked into the kitchen, and I immediately froze solid.

Then I dropped the phone.

Eventually I heard this distant voice in the ether as I waited for my mother to walk past into the laundry room, "Hello?... Hello?"

"Hello?"

"What was that?

"Hello? Cassie? Are you still there?"

"Niles?"

"Yeah...um... so, uh....I...um...was wondering if you would like to go to the shopping center with me on Saturday?"

I figured this was a good place to start for my first romantic escapade. First we would go look through the front window of the barber shop where I got my hair cut one Saturday each month.

Then, it would be on to the drugstore, where we might peruse the greeting cards and additionally see if Epsom salts might be on sale.

Then we would perhaps conclude our wonderful shopping center afternoon together by strolling past Big Wheel Car and Truck Tires and Shocks.

However, there upon in my kitchen, was dead silence for what seemed an eternity.

According to Einstein's Special Theory of Relativity, if you are in a rocket ship moving away from Earth at nearly the speed of light, time stands still. I think it is the same if you are on a phone calling up a girl for your first date.

I could barely breathe. Then, the answer came.

"No, I can't. I have to do something. I have to get something for my brother's turtle cage. Sorry."

Click.

My first ruby red luscious Adam's apple of desire had fallen from the tree, and it had a worm in it.

Cassie's response on that fateful pre-pubescent afternoon would set the pattern to similar quixotic proposals for many years to come. Sarah Jogurt made me keenly aware that this had persisted well into my twenty-seventh year, cast in stone (pottery that is).

And then there was my career. My ambitions of becoming a famous and respected avant garde composer and progressive jazz musician were stuck on fly paper. I was stranded in Nowheresville, man. I was spinning the wheels of self-expression on the gravel roads of Cowtown, USA, the home of the National Western Stock Show- Denver, Colorado. Yippee Kai Yea.

After my heroes Frank Zappa and Don Van Vliet, I had been writing modern sounding compositions and giving them such poetic titles as "Potato Chip Roundup" and "Fartsalot". I was convinced that these were immortal sonic creations. But nobody was jumping on board my musical band wagon train.

In southern California I might have met a better reception. But here, smack dab between Wichita and Salt Lake City, in Colorful Culturally Backward Colorado, someone came up to me after one of my self-promoted concerts and suggested,

"You guys would be great if you just played some *real* music."

And that comment came from one of my best friends.

I had magnificent dreams, as does every young person.

But did I know how to make those glorious dreams come true?

Heck no.

I was lost.

High school had barely prepared me to tie my own shoes.

College had shown me how to zip up my pants, and not much more.

And my parents, bless 'em, with all their honest love and guidance, still had not completely prepared me for the all important skill of *finding my own way*. Not entirely. I don't know if any parents could.

I needed my idea spark plugs re-connected.

I needed a no-fool injection.

I needed a change of under-awareness.

I needed SOMETHING.

In the summer of 1982 one evening, it came in the form of a documentary movie shown on my TV.

I had been bored out of my skull late one Saturday night, barely propping myself up in bed on my stomach, chin in one hand, remote control in the other. I was endlessly channel surfing one station after another.

Eventually I took a bathroom break at the top of the hour, got a drink of water direct from the bathroom sink faucet, returned to bed, plopped myself back down, then continued as before.

Then I saw him.

I had clicked forward to a channel coming out of a little independent nineteen-watt PBS station situated in a Quonset hut twenty miles outside of town.

I adjusted my rabbit ears and tried to get rid of as much of the furry static as I could.

On my TV set was a picture, a moving picture, a gloriously low budget faded color 16mm documentary film picture. There in the center of the screen sat this fellow, about fifty years old, on a log, in the middle of the woods.

His hair was long and nearly shoulders length. His belly button hung leisurely over the elastic band of his shorts. He wore a beard on one end and he was wearing shorts on the other. And by that I mean boxer shorts. And that was all. No shoes, no shirt. But here on educational PBS, he was supplying a service.

His hands held a one gallon bell Jar. Later I would discover how important all kinds of Jars would be in the world of Wand manipulation. But then, he held the kind of Jar that you see in a Frankenstein movie containing a brain, and that's what I saw.

In this Jar, was indeed, a brain.

And this half naked fellow was pulling this brain out of the jar, dripping wet with, I presume, formaldehyde.

Hydee hydee ho.

The brain momentarily slipped from his grip and tried to hide back inside the safety of the Jar. Plop plop. No fizz.

However, the man persisted to wrangle this creature out of its container, and moments later he proudly held up the brain at eye level. The bearded one slowly turned it to display it proudly from all 360 degrees...

"This," he said slowly, deliberately, and very grandly, "is...

"The …
Center…
Of…
The …
Universe."

Chapter 4
Dormant Brain Camp

So here is this absolutely wild looking guy holding up a dripping wet brain like a three pound mass of congealed cottage cheese looking for a home, a giant alien snail out of its shell. I sat there transfixed to my TV set, anxious to see what on Earth would come next in this obscure late night public television broadcast.

The 1970's documentary film *Stingo* was a tour de force of likely the most unusual summer camp in the history of the planet. There was a scene of songs around the crackling campfire with the director strumming his guitar. This was followed by student testimonials swearing to unbounded creativity, pleasure, and a sureness of purpose in life. Not so unusual. But then, most unusually, several subjects expounded upon newly acquired paranormal experiences such as precognition and telepathy. Another participant reported the newly found ability to peer with microscopic vision as through a high powered microscope upon one's own brain and internal organs.

This could be very handy if one were considering a surgical procedure, especially if the surgeon was a singing cowboy.

The documentary only gained steam from that point on.

The film then showed Stingo playing his folk guitar and sparring with Groucho Marx on the 1950's NBC game show *You Bet Your Life.* This classic black and white show from television's golden age was mostly a vehicle for Groucho to improvise clever quips with his as often as not quirky and unusual guest contestants. This was followed by the actual game portion where contestants were given a chance to go home with a little cash.

On that occasion Stingo perfectly played the part of a back country woodsman, complete with deer skin jacket that he claimed to have culled himself from one of his four legged friends. Groucho amusingly remarked, "If that's how you treat your friends I'd sure hate to be one of your enemies!"

I found his portrayal of an uneducated frontiersman even more amusing later on years after seeing the film of the show. I learned that in reality Stingo had attended three universities, including the University of Chicago to work on his Ph.D. But this was show business.

The comical give away for anyone in on his secret was that despite his theatrical pauses feigning complete bafflement, Stingo effortlessly and nearly instantaneously correctly answered the set of quizzicals put forth by Mr. Marx, his chosen category concerning obscure science facts. Stingo slyly won a thousand dollars for his effortless efforts.

The documentary then moved on to touch upon the numerous experimental studies done with brain lab participants. These studies scientifically documented the dramatic increases in creativity, awareness, pleasure, and improved human relations after systematically applying the lab's new techniques of brain self-control. So it was claimed.

Next in the film was a shapely and cute as a pin twenty-year-old blonde sitting by an idyllic mountain stream, all the while playing with a human skull. The top portion of the skull had neatly been fitted with hinge to allow convenient opening of the cranial cavity. She earnestly looked inside, as if hoping to re-discover a long forgotten treasure inside a sacrificial jewelry box.

What could be more fun?!

The film hammered home the inescapable message that each and every human being had been delivered upon this planet with a brain capable of infinite possibilities, and that paradoxically nearly every inhabitant of this spinning globe was using an infinitely small percentage of that potential.

Ah ha! Now I understood the facial hair- Stingo's beard was that rather uncommon fashion of Abe Lincoln; a beard minus the mustache. Stingo's very face was a subliminal Emancipation Proclamation of the Human Spirit from the Slavery of Dormant Glial Cells.

The overt purpose of the brain lab was simple: Hand each brain lab visitor an instruction manual to their own mind machine, then hand hold them through a short period of thought and behavior training during their stay at Camp Brain In Nature.

Certainly, it looked like all of the campers were having a fabulously jolly and inspiring time. This was Adventure Land for Neural Explorers. Bring your coonskin cap and a copy of Gray's Anatomy.

At the conclusion of the film, to my delight, the TV station had a live interview with the brain man himself, decked out in an out of fashion thrift store suit. Stingo and the interviewer sat on lawn chairs outside the station's half-barrel shaped army barracks, and reminisced about the origins of the brain lab.

"After my appearance on Groucho, some big New York City TV executive saw me and said, 'I know a phony when I see one, and that guy is a GREAT one...'" Stingo boasted. "So, they flew me to off to Manhattan and gave me a summer replacement show with guests like Burl Ives and Woody Guthrie."

"I played the part of a mountain man to a tee. I told back woods stories and strummed my gee-tar and sang folk songs. The network paid me $2000 an hour for the summer. At the end of the last show I looked straight into the TV camera and said, 'If anybody has a mountain to sell, call me.' And somebody did."

Stingo went on wearing a self-satisfied grin ear to ear, "I packed my bags and left the city with two grocery sacks full of money. One I gave to the IRS, and with the other one I bought Laughing Coyote Mountain."

"To this day we all work and play up on the mountain without any electricity or running water, just like my boyhood hero, explorer Jim Bridger. I live on just pennies each year, just what people donate." So that explained the out of date suit he was wearing. His budget dictated that fashion took a back seat to pick-axes and lamp oil.

Stingo then gave out a P.O. box address for correspondence and for those wanting to learn more.

Sign me up!" I shouted, standing up in my pajamas.

The postman collected my mail the next afternoon and my own letter to get directions to the brain lab was on its way. But I had much more in store for me than just simply learning about the human brain. Eventually I would learn and understand what kind of real magic Stingo had used to buy his mountain.

More than a month slowly went by, and like clockwork I had heard the familiar clank of my mailbox, day after day, but to no avail. Finally one day, my anticipation waning, I ran over to the slot in my front door and picked up the small pile of letters that lay scattered on the floor underneath.

At last! Here it was, a plain white envelope with a hand-stamped logo of a howling coyote next to the return address.

I tore open the letter and unfolded a couple of sheets. On top was a letter. Tucked behind that was another single page, briefly summarizing what I had seen on TV, with a hand drawn road map duplicated on the reverse.

I first read the simple hand typed letter with eager anticipation. The typeface indicated an old manual typewriter with a spotty ribbon, but it was personally written note specifically addressed to me:

Dear Brain Scout Niles,

Thank you for your interest in The Dormant Brain Lab. I am sure glad you enjoyed seeing the film about our work here.

Also thanks to you for patiently waiting many sunsets and moon rises for a response to your letter. Up here in the forest, I only make it down trail with my jeep to the post office box about every two weeks to roundup my mail. Then it's another two more weeks to get back to town with my gunny sack of mail going back out. In winter it's even longer when I'm snowbound and have to take the mule.

I understand your interest in learning how to better use your brain to accomplish those things important to you that you mentioned, such as personal improvement and your desire for a professional career in music.

Since 1957 we have been engaged in the systematic study and research of the most fabulous instrument in the known universe: The Human Brain. I would suggest that better use of this In-Your-Head-strument would help you in achieving your goals, and more.

We have visitors come here from all over the world each summer, and I cordially invite you to come visit our facility at your convenience any Sunday afternoon between the hours of noon and five P.M. Please see the enclosed mimeograph sheet for map, directions and a guide for visitors. You need only bring your brain and your willingness to learn.

Yours Sincerely,
D.A.T. Stingo, Director
Dormant Brain Research and Development Lab
Laughing Coyote Mtn., Blackhawk, Colorado

Stingo's response was a curious combination of back-woods twang and serious science, and I had never seen anything like it before.

I was raring to go. The very next Saturday, I packed my backpack with a peanut butter sandwich, a thermos full of hot tea, hopped in my car, then took off.

BOW WOW 2
I Am Not A Guy

Everything that follows hinges upon THIS very first lesson, for it is the basis of the power that one manipulates with one's Wand.

And this is what I, The Book of Wands, am all about:
Traveling with the aid and use of a Wand.

And what IS Travel?

This is easy, yet difficult. Anything that I say Traveling is, is not Traveling.

Certainly you cannot contain Travel or anything else for that matter in mere symbols that mean something else. A representation of anything- IS NOT THAT THING, so obviously.

However, this record, in its entirety will provide a general approximation for the meaning of Travel. Eventually, at some point after ingestion of this collected symbolic representations of ideas, those predisposed to experience the actual thing, the essence of Travel, will utter, "Ah ha!".

What I must emphasize is that I do not mean for you to mistake that somewhere generating this tome I was initially sitting around, a tube of mortal skin and bone, a walking food processor with eyes and clumsy fingers and a big shiny nose.

I am happy to report that has not been my package previous, not then, not now, and will not be so in the future.

I lounge comfortably beyond scratch marks made by mechanical Pencil or Typewriter, quill pen or charcoal on cave wall, past any scribbling made by a common three dimensional collection of self-mobile cells that you may perceive as an initiator of paragraphs.

Am I making myself clear?

I am not the result of some GUY writing a book,

Rather, I am

Original Idea and Thought

flying boundless above the common chlorinated swimming pool of popular perception.

I.e., I, the true "author" of this book, The Book of Wands, I am not a person, the creation of a person, nor the product of writer with or without a contract, but a growing idea, a moving concept

Such is your's truly,
The Book of Wands.

Like any living creature, even though you can reread this sentence a thousand times, I am not static. Rather, I am as changeable as a bank of white clouds drifting against a carpet of blue. There you see me. There you don't. I move. I Travel.

My Mind Mine bubbles out a new synthetic vision reflected in these particular printed words. But, I am a creative un-embodied entity, merely dressed in the form of whatever you happen to have there speaking to you.

This book is a convenient footprint left in the sand.

Follow it as far as you can. My trail will lead to the edge of the water only, my impression then to be found washed away in the ocean of daily infinities.

To go on, you must dive in and swim from a defined sandy shore and leave the beached whales of conformity behind. Otherwise, you will remain just another Lump of slimy rock moss.

I am out of the reach of most of you, and not because you can't touch your toes.

I am, in fact, right here.

To shake my hand, you must learn to pass through the cheese grate where there is no grate.

Although any two of us are like un-matchable evanescent snowflakes, as the Universe was created from one super compressed infinitely dense spot one Big Bang Afternoon, you and I are forever Cosmic Dust Bunny Cousins, made from the very same unitary polka dot. No matter how many galaxies you hop, skip, and jump away, I'm there right next to you, sharing your ancestral spiral twisted pretzel DNA blue jeans and squeezed right in next to you, between you and your underwear.

Smmmmmmmmmmmmmmmmmmmmoooooch.

And that's how it ALL is, all of the time.

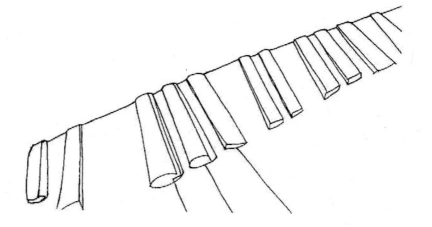

Chapter 5
Riddle of the Ph.B.

The drive to Laughing Coyote Mountain consisted of a hop, skip, and a jump west into the foothills from my urban stomping grounds, winding forty miles deep on the two lane blacktop of U.S. 6 through historic Clear Creek Canyon. Many miles further south was the newer six-lane Interstate 70 that took the brunt of most of the mountain traffic. The old highway now saw much less use, and most of that was for Sunday picnics with grandma and the kiddies.

U.S. Pot Hole 6 east of the old mining towns of Central City and Blackhawk was bordered much of the way on the shoulder by gold tailings from the Colorado gold rush days, like endless giant anthills one after another for miles on end. I wondered if I would find another kind of gold at the end of my journey on that afternoon.

I kept my eyes peeled for a raccoon tail hanging on a sign marking the Smith Hill Road turn off, just as Stingo's hand drawn mimeographed map indicated. I easily passed it on my first and second try. When I finally found it, the small wooden road sign was nearly falling off its post, and either a tourist or a cougar had made off with the tail.

The little gravel lane quickly turned my car into the inside of a washing machine with me as the dirty socks, so bad were the washboard ruts that went on endlessly from the beginning. I was sure I would spot errant pieces of my station wagon randomly scattered about on the return trip.

Although the drive off of the main road was initially as horizontally level as the paved highway that I had been on, within minutes it quickly became steep and narrow. A thick dark pine tree forest laced with patches of lighter green flickering aspen bordered the road on either side. The dirt road wound on and on for miles, then finally split at a fork in the road just past a small uninhabited volunteer fire station, an inconspicuous tiny red garage with a small water tank tower nearly hidden in the trees.

There was absolutely no other sign of civilization at this point, and even the fire station looked like ruins from a long lost world. I looked at the map and paused.

You know what they say, "When you come to a fork in the road, eat." So I pulled out the parking brake, pulled out my lunch, and sat down next to my car. My eyes took in the high mountain meadow scenery while my stomach took in a peanut butter and jelly sandwich.

Before long I was on my way again. The road abruptly became viciously ever more steep at this point, my car tires struggling to find grip on billions of loose gravel ball bearings. My old Datsun station wagon was not a motorized mountain goat, this became strikingly clear.

Nevertheless, I threw my car into first gear, kicked up a pile of dust behind me, and managed to slip-slide it past the rise. I would later learn that in winter this portion of road was completely impassable in nothing less than a four-wheeled drive jeep with chains- or else a good pair of neoprene soled hiking boots.

A quarter-mile later the road leveled out again having gained perhaps a fifteen-hundred feet or more above Clear Creek, now far away and below. As I glanced out the window I could see the Continental Divide in the distance along with fourteen-thousand foot high Pikes Peak sixty miles downwind and an even higher Mt. Evanescence across the valley. The view was dizzy and splendiferous.

Suddenly some fuzzy crazy zig-zagging thing crossed the road ten feet in front of me and I jammed on the brakes. Like a flash, it disappeared into the trees instantly.

I thought that maybe I was seeing things. As a decent biology student in high school I was familiar with native wildlife. That thing, what two-second glance I had been given, looked like nothing I could identify. I dismissed my brief hallucination as the effect of thin air and altitude. Perhaps it was an omen of stranger things to come.

I drove on in the flickering sunlight that strobe-painted the surface of the dirt road. Finally, at long last I spotted a modest stone gate and a cast iron plate marking the entrance to the brain lab. These were the last remnants of a long dismembered and grander wooden and stone arch that I had just seen in Stingo's TV documentary that had been produced only ten years earlier. The now missing archway had originally proclaimed the lab's existence in a more conspicuous fashion. Now, the eighteen-inch-wide plate embedded amongst the remains of a stone wall was all that was left.

The plate read, "Founded 1957, D.A. Stingo, PH.B., B.Sci., M.A., Director" What the heck was a *Ph.B,* ? I hadn't heard of that before. Was this one of Stingo's jokes? A typo hammered in steel, too inconvenient to replace? Was someone handing out a Doctor of Brain degree?

It turns out that I would stare at the sign and ponder that riddle unsolved for a full twenty-five years.

Eventually I figured it out, and the solution took mere seconds. From that point on, just glancing at images of this sign would forever remind me of the inherent human tendency for inertia. Since I answered that silly nagging intellectual mosquito bite many years ago, I've nailed a photo of it to my refrigerator to keep me on my toes. Apparently, outgrowing laziness never ceases, even for brain lab graduates.

Et tu?

I backed my car up a little bit and looked for a gap in the trees, the inconspicuous entrance to the so-called "parking lot" as indicated on the map. Neither an asphalt or even a dirt lot, this was a small grass meadow hidden from the road, and required a very confident driver willing to drive his wheels over a small ditch, some very sharp rocks, and a few pointy fallen branches.

Sighing a breath of relief at finding all of my tires absent any new puncture wheezings, I locked my car. I did not want my car radio stolen by some unexpectedly dexterous brown bear.

At one end of the meadow I could spot an old worn and rusty hand water pump. I presumed that the narrow trail leading up from there led to the brain lab proper.

I trudged up the nearly invisible dirt path. At many places it was no more than an inches-wide trail of depressed grass. It made the previous road look tame by comparison and it truly seemed nearly vertical at many points. I had to stop over and over again to catch my breath and to catch a tree branch to keep me from falling on my city slicker butt.

It was beautiful wall to wall rocks, grass, trees, and wildflowers at every turn of the head. And the smell of the air was divine.

"So *that's* what clean air smells like," I thought.

Immediately there was a remarkable quietude present that I had never experienced any where else in my life. Normally for any city dweller, the absence of sound only exists within four walls of one sort or another of a sound proof chamber, or with the use of ear plugs. Here I found the same absolute quiet as one might find inside a stainless steel bank vault, but I was in the middle of natural abundance everywhere.

The setting was unique for me. I was in the middle of everything, and everything made virtually no sound at all.

Then, more curiously, I began to notice something quite unusual. I could hear a steady background drone inside my head, a steady beat less

rooooooooohhhhhhhhhhhhhhhhhhmmmmmmmmm

I was stumped. So, I sat down *on* a stump trying to figure out what the mysterious humming was and where it was coming from.

"What is that?" I thought.

It was *weird*.

Suddenly it dawned on me. I put my hands over my ears, closed my eyes, and listened intently.

"Wow," I realized, "That's the echo of my car engine still bouncing around inside my head!" I had never noticed such a sound before, even after driving for hours. But here in the forest where there was barely any sound at all, this internal reverberation was as plain as day. The lack of cityscape background noises in the utterly natural landscape made me sensitive to something I had always missed before: Inter-cranial Engine Afterburn.

In retrospect, I would discover that this new found sensitivity was at the crux of many brain lab experiences. The remote virgin forest, away from all the manner of civilized distractions, gave one an unparalleled new perspective and sensitivity to one's interior self and one's exterior You-niverse. This would be a key in later experimentation properly guiding Unusual Tools, tools that nobody else would even admit existed.

As I learned with each new visit to Stingo's mountain retreat, you could experience things at The Dormant Brain Lab that you could not duplicate anywhere else. Here I would find just the right combination of natural solitude blended with just the right amount of creature comforts.

Unlike fasting for forty days in the desert until you were as thin as a toothpick, or a year spent meditating in a damp wet cave, the brain lab offered clean mountain water, a small grocery store maybe forty minutes away, the safety of a log cabin, and a wood stove for drying your muddy wet shoes after a thunderstorm.

Why sleep on a sticky bed of nails when you could have an old mattress on a log floor for the same price?

In the late 60's and early 70's, i.e. in the Summer of Love and slightly beyond, one brand or another of Guru-ism was *the thing* in pop culture. Grand Masters of This and That popped up on every corner.

71

But The Age of Aquarius was frequently blended with cold cash Madison Avenue commercialism more times than not. In those days, and even still quite common, various spiritual organizations as well as independent and institutional education and research was often run with a level of opportunism, dogma, authoritarianism, and ruthless hierarchy that would make a Roman emperor blush.

By contrast, Stingo decidedly took a back seat to the master of your brain, and that was YOU. For a six week intensive course that included rugged home cooked vegetarian meals, you paid only what you could afford, and at the most this was a couple hundred bucks- the paper kind, that is, not the kind with antlers.

You paid for your expenses and contributed to help satisfy Stingo's endless need for postage stamps. In return, you got a custom fitted program of *brain self-control.* The lab director provided experience, guidance and a tested regimen of study.

But essentially every participant was his or her own boss all the way. Stingo was The Anti-guru. He frequently made this perfectly clear with a hearty self-depreciating giggle, "Your way is not my way, and *my way is certainly is not your way!*"

But all of that was still unknown to me.

This was my first visit. I made my way slowly up the mountain side and at last arrived behind a rickety log structure with a red tar paper roof that extended from the top of the A-frame all the way down to the dirt and weeds.

I walked around to the front and found myself at a small clearing perhaps half an acre in size. It was occupied by a tilled garden plot located downhill, another smaller cabin fifty yards away, the wreck of a roofless uncompleted log structure in the shadow of some trees, another hand water pump up the hill about fifty feet, and an old pale blue army jeep at the end of a dirt path that nearly qualified for a road. This must have been the end of the road that started from behind the stone gate that I had seen upon my arrival.

At the summit of the roof of this first little cabin was an old rusty brown school bell. From it hung a rope that brushed the ground.

The small cabin's entrance lie a few wooden steps down in the dirt, the door a simple unpainted wooden affair with a glass window cracked in one corner. Next to the door was a bulletin board with a few odd scraps of paper and a big hand written note, written upon it with a bold black magic marker in crooked lettering, "Ring Bell 10 times and I'll whistle you on up."

I wasn't ready to announce my presence yet, because I first wanted to look around a little bit in private. I walked down the steps and peered inside the window.

Inside was a stove, a few odds and ends like enamel pots and pans, some dishes, and a few boxes. This was a primitive back woods kitchen, surely. The window ledge was a mausoleum for flies.

Eek. Either wilderness housekeeping was a low priority relative to brain work, or it was just plain impossible to maintain the same level of cleanliness as one might in a suburban cooking zone.

I walked around the outside of this cabin, the walls protected by the long extended roof. There was lots of firewood, and shovels and axes hanging on big nails hammered into the side of the logs that made up the walls.

There were sticks everywhere, piled up like firewood, but curiously not at all like logs- they were too skinny for that. "Kindling?" I thought. The sticks were made from tree branches, some of them stripped clean of their bark, others waiting. Some were six feet long, others mere inches. I assumed "tent posts" and other things I could not fathom, and left it at that.

But most unusually, the log walls under the protection of the A-frame roof were absolutely covered- littered one might say- with hand written notes, woodland graffiti of a strange sort.

"Lone Wolf- BINC 1972- Never lonely again!" stated one signatory.

"Lost since birth, finally FOUND- April May Flower, June '69", signed another.

"City Smog Sucks - Mountain Air Breathes- Dragon Dan, BINC '75"

Such was an obvious ritual of brain lab participants; to leave their fingerprint permanently on the very walls of the establishment. It was unique and quite unexpected.

Then there was a funny little cartoon, maybe seven inches across, simply drawn of a sheep herder standing with a long staff next to one of his sheep. The caption read "H.I.S. L.A.B.M. >>>>" with little arrows pointing off in the opposite direction of the clearing, off to the west away from the center of the camp.

"Ha, somebody can't spell!" I said out loud. I glanced off in the direction of the arrow, but saw nothing but trees and more trees. I saw no furry sheep or even one little lamb.

I continued scanning the wall graffiti and came upon another scribbling that caught my attention…

"Always take spare jeep keys to town- D.A. Stingo, June 68".

I walked completely around and found myself at the dangling bell rope, grabbed it, and pulled hard. Nothing. The bell was stuck.

I looked up to see what the hang up was, and tried tugging from an oblique angle in the opposite direction…

"DONG!!!!" it came unstuck and rang out suddenly and clearly.

"Wow..", I had never done this before in my life, rung an actual school bell. Five minutes at the lab and I was already involved in a brand new adventure. I felt like a teacher in a Lucy Maud Montgomery novel, expecting a little red haired girl to coming running by any moment.

"DING!!! DING!!! DING!!! DING!!!"

I listened. Oh yeah, ten times…

DING!!! DING!!! DING!!! DING!!!"

DING!!! DING!!! DING!!!"

Oops.

I listened carefully.

Nothing.

Then more nothing

Then I heard a "Woot woot woot" loud hoot-owl human whistle uphill behind me, from the trees, farther up the trail. It seemed a couple of hundred yards away.

"Up here! COME UP HERE!!"

"Woot Woot Woot!!!!!!!!"

I took a deep breath and headed uphill. Towards what, I did not know.

I had no idea what a Wand was. I didn't even know that they existed. Controlling them would come eventually. But first I would have to learn about the organic machine that did the controlling. And that was a major adventure in itself.

Chapter 6
Buckets and Brains

I started climbing up the brain lab mountain in the direction of the hoot owl call that I had heard just moments before. I slowly wound above the clearing via a steep curving path cut into the side of the hill that threaded its way past fallen pine trees and small boulders. Finally, about a hundred or so feet ahead and above me at the point where the trail vanished, there stood D.A.T. Stingo, waving.

"Up here!" he shouted. "Come on up," he added as he turned and walked beyond my line of sight.

As I made it to the top of the trail, I could just see Stingo disappear inside another cabin that sat precariously on the side of the hill a little further back.

This cabin also had a roof that went from its peak down to the forest floor, but this was only on one side of the building. This roof side was completely covered with dirt and sod, and one haphazard skylight.

On the opposite side, the cabin faced the south with nearly a full wall of crooked slap-dashed glass windows. I imagined that with the spectacular view that I now saw in front of me, this was as much for scenery as it was for solar rays.

On this cabin, the door was painted bright red with a large nicely quartered glass window in the center. As Stingo came back outside, I noticed that he had to crouch down to get through. He looked like a giant leaving a cottage that belonged to the seven dwarves.

"Sit down, sit down," Stingo instructed as he pointed to one of two large split logs situated a few feet from the cabin's entrance.

I started to sit down and he held my arm. "Not here, you sit on that one," he pointed, "So you can have the view." One bench sat at a ninety degree angle to the other, the second bench with a clear view of the range of mountains that lay grandly across the valley.

He started buttoning up an old flannel shirt that he had obviously just put on for guest company. Underneath he wore an old pair of boxer shorts.

I had not said a word. I don't know if it was telepathy or not, but Stingo knew that I had noticed the door.

He pointed behind himself at the cabin without turning to look at it. "When I started out, I brought up kids from juvenile hall down in the city, and they'd never seen a pine cone in their life. They helped me build this cabin as part of their outdoors training. But they made the door for somebody their own size, " he lightly chuckled.

He finished buttoning his shirt, and then smacked and licked his lips, like a hungry wolf about to devour his innocent prey. He then looked me straight in the eye. "What are you doing here?" he suddenly asked quite sternly.

I was taken aback as this was really not the genial tone I had expected at all. He wasn't smiling at all now.

I reached into my pocket and took out the letter and the map he had sent to me in the mail.

"Um, I'm Niles Abercrumby, and you sent me this." I held up the letter somewhat sheepishly for him to see. "I came up to see what you do here. At the lab."

Stingo rubbed his eyes, scrunched his mouth, and paused for a moment as if irritated. Then he continued with a decidedly unforgiving tone, "The first thing you learn around here is to READ and follow the instructions." His gaze was piercing, and he spoke slowly and deliberately, *"You didn't follow the instructions."*

"Huh?" I answered quietly. I started pouring over the sheet I had brought with me to see what I had missed. "It said between noon…" He didn't let me finish.

"We don't have visitors *today*," he glared. "READ THE INSTRUCTIONS."

I frantically scanned the letter. But before I finished, Stingo scolded, "Today's Saturday, not Sunday. Sunday is for visitors. NOT Saturday."

I started to get up to leave. "Oh, sorry…"

"No, no, sit down, sit down," he reluctantly insisted. "You're already here." He waved me back down towards the log.

He continued, "On Saturday I'm completely in my frontal lobes flow. Visitors bring all their city chaos with them, and if I'm not ready for it, it's a mess. Their entropy slops up everything. I have to be ready for all their confusion." Stingo then dusted off his legs with his hands.

He sighed, and then seemed to relax a bit and consign himself to the situation, i.e., *me* disturbing his "flow". He grabbed up a little twig off the end of his log, and started to casually pick his teeth.

There was a decidedly awkward pause in the conversation. I didn't know what to say, although I now realized I had gotten the day wrong. Otherwise, I had hardly understood what he was talking about.

He went on, starting anew, "Okay, so tell me, what do you need?"

"Oh gosh," I thought for a moment, then blurted out the obvious, or so I thought. "I just wanted to see what you did up here, and what this place…"

He quickly interrupted me again. "No, no, no. What do you *need*?"

I didn't understand the question.

"What do you NEED?" he asked again, "Tell me what you *NEED*."

My mouth hung open slightly as I tried to figure out exactly what he was getting at. I didn't say I needed anything actually. If I didn't come there to check out the grounds, he must have been referring to something else. And I was missing it.

"What do I *need*?" I questioned half under my breath. I nervously started to chew on my index fingernail.

Suddenly I heard this rustle and noise in the trees nearby, and a gust of wind began to blow things around. It came out of nowhere.

Stingo picked up his chin and looked around. He seemed to be noting something that I could not perceive. Suddenly, something darted through the brush near the back side of the cabin. Was it one of those odd creatures I saw on the road coming darting out again?

"What was that?" I exclaimed.

"Nothing, nothing," Stingo dismissed, and he looked around a bit, almost like an owl pivoting its head and observing

I suddenly had the feeling that the forest wind was mirroring back my own inner nervous discomfort.

Stingo silently bobbed his head as if in recognition. "Mmmmm," he said quietly.

Then he faced directly back towards me.

"Come on, what do you need? Again…"

Stingo sat there studying me. I felt like an insect under a magnifying glass.

I tried to concentrate on an answer. "Um… I need to be happy?" I suggested, holding my breath.

"Good, good." Stingo said. "That's a start. What else?"

I was a bit relieved and exhaled. "Let's see," I pondered with a pause. Finally I blurted out again, not quite sure, "I need to be a good musician?"

"Are you certain?" he asked.

I lifted my eyebrows.

"You would *like* to be a good musician. But are you absolutely certain you *need* to be?"

This question stopped my thoughts. I had simply taken this assumption for granted after playing music all of my life. "I *think* I need to be a musician. I *like* being a musician," I answered.

"Not the same," he said. "Go on."

I had to think for a few moments. Then with hesitation and some embarrassment I admitted, "Um… I want to be loved… by this girl. This girl I broke up with… ?"

I said this, hoping it was the right answer. But with a sinking gut I knew the chances of that was about as slim as one of the blades of wild buffalo grass trapped under my foot.

Stingo shook his head like he had already anticipated my reply. Did he know that I was talking about the girl who had ripped my heart out just months ago? Or had he heard this confession so many times that it didn't matter who the girl was...

"Do you love *yourself?*" Stingo struck back.

"Huh?"

Then I began to feel like an even smaller insect captured under a microscope, never mind under a harmless magnifying glass. I could sense a mounting pin poised above my quivering thorax. Here I was getting a full psychological examination and the wood log under my butt wasn't even warm yet. I squirmed in my seat.

"*Do you love yourself?!*" Stingo emphatically asked again

"I guess. I suppose I do," I replied meekly.

"I suppose? How do you expect anyone to love you if you don't love yourself?"

Well, it was obvious to *him.*

Dr. Sigmund Stingo was giving me a third degree barbequing and pouring on the hot sauce. He relentlessly hammered on, "Go on, what *else* do you need?"

I just sat. I couldn't think of anything. I was speechless. I was more in shock than anything. Stingo had completely dispensed with the common cultural oilings that strangers generally engage in upon first meeting. This was not whiffle ball. This was hard ball.

I just arched my eyebrows in helplessness.

"Okay," he said. "That's fine for now."

I breathed a sigh of relief.

He went on, "If you want to control your life, you must first learn to control the thinking meat inside your skull. And to do that, you must first learn how your brain works. Follow me."

"Uh oh," I thought.

Stingo pushed himself up.

I followed him through the tiny door and into the cabin.

Inside the cabin, I looked around. It was at most about fifteen feet across in either direction, and about the same in height. There was actually very little free floor space. A full sized bed with an old mattress covered by an old faded spread out sleeping bag took up nearly half of the place.

In one corner was a large sky blue enameled wood stove with the name "Universal" in big letters on the front. In two other corners were several file cabinets. Against the inside of the glass walled side of the cabin was a mimeograph machine and shelves with supplies of all sorts; tape, paper, Pens, Pencils, ink, Staplers, and so on.

Smack dab in the middle of the cabin were two standing tree trunks, one in the corner with its bark intact, the other smack in the middle of the cabin with all of its branches and bark stripped down smooth. It was obvious that both trees helped to supply support for the roof. The trunk in the middle was a virtual bulletin board, covered with more magic marker notes, notably names of people. These names were all in the same handwriting, unlike the cook's cabin graffiti, and presumably the work of Stingo.

And then there were the walls. In a few vacant spots were nails upon which hung a wide variety of knick knacks like Rulers, a protractor, a few aluminum pots, and eating utensils. Again, as on the outside of the cook's cabin, there was writing everywhere. But here all the writing was pinned to the inside walls upon scores of index card notes. Some of it was in plain English, but much of it was in some cryptic foreign tongue with fancy curly cue letters in all colors and oddball symbols that could have passed for chemistry and physics formulae.

Beyond all of this, the great majority of wall space inside from the ceiling rafters all the way down to the stone floor was completely covered in books. There was shelf after shelf of books and books and books of all shape, color, and sizes.

Every couple of feet scattered here and there on the front part of each shelf was stuck a hand written label, each apparently describing the content of the reading material above. Again, many of these labels were in strange lettering.

Stingo picked up a foot-high hand-made pine footstool from the corner and placed it on the dusty floor in front of me, then motioned me to sit down. He fluffed up a couple of old pillows on the bed and reclined back down himself, hands and fingers laced behind his head.

"What's that language?" I asked, pointing to the numerous labels and writing.

"Oh that?" Stingo smiled. "I learned Russian in World War II. Our allies then, you know? Now I use it to keep sharp. It makes me work to remember what I wrote. I continuously challenge myself. I don't want to grow cobwebs in my ears." He took his pinkie, stuck it out at a right angle, and scratched the inside of his ear.

"Oh," I nodded.

"Besides, I need to keep some things to myself, especially when I have people up here that I don't know very well, and people I don't trust." Stingo nonchalantly glanced out the big picture window.

Was he referring to me?

I looked up and spotted a couple of what looked like guitar cases above me in a little bunk loft high up. On the edge of the loft platform was a particularly ornate and cryptic label. I thought that these items must have been something particularly special.

"So, Niles, my good new friend, where did you go to school?" This seemed to be moving in a deliberately more casual tone.

"Downtown. Metro State College," I answered.

"Uh huh. And what did they teach you about the human brain?" he asked.

"I took a biology course, but we didn't study the human brain much, " I said.

"Of course, of course," Stingo replied, my answer apparently expected.

"When you go to college, your brain is like a ten-cylinder motor running on two cylinders. You graduate, you get a diploma, and they never even bother to teach you how to connect the other eight spark plugs." He sucked on his teeth.

I was trying to imagine having spark plug wires inside my head.

Stingo went on, "That's what we do here. You teach yourself how to connect all the cylinders. You've been crawling along like a snail most of your life because nobody took the time to help you learn how to use the most important organ in your body. Your friends didn't tell you, your parents didn't show you, and your teachers at school certainly didn't help you with it."

He scratched his head. "Actually, now that I think about it, I'm wrong. You go in with two connected, and in college they pull off the last two. Hahah!" He laughed heartily.

Stingo swept across the air with his arm, "The human brain has infinite potential. Yet, despite everything we know, the human brain remains 90% dormant."

I saw the space inside my own head as one big vacuum, then retorted, "Hey, I thought that was just a myth?" I answered. "I've heard that's just a saying, it's not really true."

"No, no," Stingo closed his eyes and shook his head. "Here," he said as he suddenly sat up. He stood up upon his bed, which sunk even further with his standing weight, and began rifling through some loose papers high on one of the shelves above the mattress. A few narrow little sticks were knocked off the shelf. They looked liked fancy chop sticks, with colorful designs painted on them, but I couldn't figure on Stingo bringing much Chinese take-out up there. Stingo quickly scooped them up and put them back up on the shelf, tucking them out of sight.

"Let's see, where is that…. Ah ha!"

He removed a small pile of papers, leafing through them. "Uh huh…mmmmm…ah!"

He pulled out one sheet then sat back down on the mattress cross legged, then pointed to the page, printed proof as to what he would next declare.

"We do not know what human beings are fully capable of. This is what Sir John Eccles said, and he won the Noble Prize." Stingo began reading the quotation,

"All indications point to the conclusion that the brain and its powers are endless."

He turned the page towards me for emphasis, then exclaimed with loud drama, "If the human brain has endless capacity, how do you measure a percentage of infinity?!"

I had to work this out in my head, and I was having a little trouble on my own. Maybe it was the altitude.

"Even if you are using 99% of your brain, what is 99% of infinity? It's nothing! It's an infinitely small slice of an infinitely big pie!" He continued to fling his hands and the flapping pages around in exclamation.

"The whole idea that you are using all of your brain or any percentage for that matter is completely absurd. Heck, even the idea that you are using 10% of your brain is too generous. The point is," he said pointing again to the papers, "The folksy notion that you are using only a smidgen of what you are capable of is intuitively *correct*. People correctly intuit that they are not even getting out of first gear!"

He leaned closer towards me. "Tell me Niles… *exactly what are you capable of?*" His eyebrows lifted high.

"If you can tell me that, I'll tell you that you're using more than 10% of your brain!" He pointed in the air like an orator making an important point

"People don't have a clue about how their brain works. And if you don't know how the motor works, where the brake is, where to put the key, where to put the gas and the oil, how to change gears- you're not going to get anywhere, *no matter what other TOOLS you might have in that trunk."*

He emphasized this last fact by gently poking his fingertip right on my forehead.

"Tools? What tools?" I had the feeling he was talking about something I didn't quite get yet. What tools was he referring to?

Ignoring my question he continued unabated, "Once you learn how this engine works, once you learn a few brain basics and apply them, then..."

Stingo slapped his hands together ten inches from my face and moved one hand zapping off like a rocket sled-

"Then...BANG! ZOOOOOMMMMMM!!!!"

He relaxed, and reclined back in his bed.

He laughed and spoke in an assured jolly tone, waving his hand leisurely in the air, "No more grinding gears, no more flat tires. Life becomes an infinitely interesting game with the universe. It flows from one moment to the next, like a well oiled machine."

My heart was beating fast. This guy was *good.* Stingo had delivered with impressive panache, like a well rehearsed actor. My mind was racing with the mere idea that my brain, my very own brain was boundless. Nobody had suggested that to me before.

"So," he said gazing at the ceiling, "Do you want to learn?"

"Oh yeah... yes," I said excitedly, "This sounds great!"

"Alright then." Stingo sat back up and stepped off the bed and over to the stove. Next to it sat a galvanized steel bucket with a handle.

"This is your second lesson." He sat back on the bed in front of me, bucket in hand.

"My *second* lesson?" I asked, perplexed. "I'm confused."

"Yes, your second one. What was your first lesson?"

I had to think.

"Oh yeah," I admitted. "Always read the instructions."

"Correct," Stingo lightly agreed. "Now this is part deux."

I anxiously waited, and couldn't for the life of me figure out what the bucket was for. Maybe I was supposed to go out and gather some special rocks outside. I had no idea.

Stingo spoke as if he had said these lines a thousand times, perfectly rehearsed and repeated to countless students. "The human brain is three brains in one. It is known as a Triune brain, tri- meaning three, -une meaning one. Three in one. Three brains in one."

"Okay, I get that," I said softly. That was easy.

"It is a reptile brain seed surrounded by a mammal brain core. Then these two parts are further enveloped by a thick advanced primate brain."

"Okay." I was following this elementary brain physiology lesson without too much problem. So far so good.

"Here," Stingo said, putting the bucket down next to me and then reaching over to grab a fresh green apple that was sitting on the edge of a shelf next to an old worn copy of *Fun With Dick and Jane*, the original elementary school reader that I had myself used in the first grade. Perhaps quite an appropriate coincidence.

He grabbed an impressive looking 10-inch long antler handled Bowie knife that was hanging by a thick piece of rope on a nail hammered into the log wall.

Stingo carefully cut the apple in half as I looked on. He pointed to the inside of the apple with the tip of the huge knife, and said as he first indicated to the seeds, then to the core, and then to the big juicy white flesh of the apple, "Reptile brain, mammal brain, primate brain."

He first offered me one half of the apple and took a loud crunchy bite out of the other half himself.

"Thanks," I said, and I took a bite myself.

Stingo put his piece of the apple down on the bed. "In order to control your brain and get the most out of it you must understand how each of these independent parts of the brain work. Each layer has specific functions, but each can work together to one extent or another with the other layers."

He again seemed to emphasize this next point, "What ever you do in life, what you do with other tools that you use, no matter how unusual that tool, it always comes back to what part of your brain is actually wielding such a Wan..." He stopped in mid sentence, then cleared his throat. "It always comes back to what part of your brain is actually manipulating such a *tool*." He held up the knife in front of me and paused as if wanting me to contemplate the last sentence. "You got that?"

"Sure," I responded hopefully. "I think so."

But I wasn't really quite exactly sure what he meant. I was actually more pre-occupied with the big knife.

"The reptile brain can do nothing but kill as a murderer with the same knife that the frontal lobes will use to heal, like a surgeon." He hung up the knife while I pondered what he had just said. I actually was relieved that he was putting the weapon away out of immediate reach.

"The reptile brain- It computes basic survival: Feeding, Fighting, Fleeing, and you know, basic stuff."

"Oh yeah," I scoured my mind, "Basic. Stuff."

Stingo continued the lesson. "The mammal brain layer adds on rudimentary social interaction, nurturing, emotion..."

"Warm fuzzies," I added.

"Exactly. Cooperative consciousness. But that's just half of the time. The other half of the time the mammal brain clicks backward into full *competitive* consciousness, back into the reptile brain. Then it's pure dog eat dog."

I nodded my head agreeably, apparently with my mammal brain.

"Alright then. The problem for most humans is that they barely click much past the first or second layers, the reptile and the mammal brain. And that's a shame, because the juiciest part is right here, in the primate brain." Stingo poked my forehead with his finger with distinctly more pressure this time. I was glad he wasn't poking at me with the tip of the knife.

"This is your *frontal lobes*, click your amygdala forward out of your reptile brain and into your frontal lobes, and that's when the magic happens. You pop your frontals."

Now he was starting to lose me again. "Amygdala?" "Click?" "Pop?" I thought to myself. This sounded more like a demented Rice Crispies cereal commercial. Was he going to wire me up? Was he going to put an implant in my brain with a toggle switch connected? Was my brain going to explode? The images in my own brain were starting to make me nervous.

Stingo then held out his palm in front of me. "Now, take your hand like this and grab your whole forehead... spread out all your fingers." Stingo turned his palm around grabbed his own forehead, and waited for me to imitate him, which I did.

He went on, "Everything under your hand is the most advanced part of your brain, your frontal lobes. It does things no other part can do. It's the cosmic cranial treasure chest. The Big Kahuna. It's where the infinity jackpot is found."

"Uh…" I grappled with the concept as I grappled my head..

"But the cosmic joke is that it's mostly dormant. It's turned off. It's locked up. The electricity hardly ever gets that far. ZZZZTTTT! The road's blocked. Short circuit, broken connection." Stingo made a quick cut-throat gesture with the side of his hand in front of his own throat.

I lurched back reactively.

"Good," Stingo nodded. "Now, put your thumbs in your ears."

"Eh?"

"Put your thumbs in your ears, like this…" Stingo stuck his thumbs, one in each ear, with his palms facing forward, fingers extended. It looked like he had big mouse ears. I copied the motion.

Stingo then grasped his head between his fingers, the thumb in the ear, the middle finger in the side corner of each eye. Again, I copied his hand work.

"Now," he said, "Drape your pointer finger down the side of your head, like this," which he did, "...'Till its right in between the other two fingers- and POINT!" At the word 'point', Stingo dramatically pointed in at his temples.

But I didn't follow suit. "You didn't say Simon Says." I smiled.

Stingo smiled sarcastically. "Okay wise guy... Simon says... Point!"

I pointed.

"One inch inside your skull, right smack in the middle of your meat motor, one for each side of your brain is your main brain gear shift lever..." Stingo pretended to shift a car shifter. "Your internal wizard's staff." Stingo then motioned as if he was holding a Wand.

I shook my head from side to side and indicated, "I don't get it..."

He elaborated, "Your Magic Master Click Switch... your *amygdala*." Again, he reached behind onto the shelf right above his bed. Next to another well worn ragged copy of a book that had "Tesla" on it's spine he grabbed a big brown plastic electrical toggle switch. He held it up and clicked it back and forth several times, making a loud clicking noise.

"Ah-mig-doll-uh," he said slowly.

"Migdolluh," I responded.

"Click click click. You click energy forward from where it is stuck in your primitive reptile brain forward to the most advance part of your brain, right behind your eyebrows. Click your amygdala. Do that enough Mr. Abercrumby, and when you do, you'll pop your frontals."

Again, I raised my eyebrows with my fingers still in my ears. I didn't get it. Amygdala, click, pop- Stingo sounded more like a mad elf and a whole lot less like a brain researcher. Stingo reached up and gently pushed my hands down.

"Okay, okay," he said, noting the confusion on my face.

"Um, I'm not sure… frontal lobe, mammal brain, reptile brain… I'm a person…" I admitted my puzzlement.

Stingo put the switch back carefully on the shelf. He put the unfinished apple over on the stove and picked up the bucket that he had sat down on the floor next to me. "Put this on your head."

"Huh?" I exclaimed.

"Put this over your head."

I slowly took the bucket from Stingo and reluctantly held it above my head.

"No," he said. "Not above your head. Turn it around and cover your head. Everyone who comes up to the lab does this. This is your catechism. Go on." He grabbed the bucket, flipped it over, and gave it back to me.

Suddenly I nervously felt that things were decidedly taking a turn for the worst, and I began to seriously doubt my decision to trek up to this place. He seemed as mad as the Mad Hatter.

"Go on. Or go home," Stingo drew the line. He meant business.

I paused for a moment and thought, "What have I gotten myself into…" I then slowly lowered the bucket over my entire head and held on to the edges. It was nearly pitch black.

"Say, 'Me me me!'" Stingo commanded.

"What?" I answered, my own voice metallically reverberating inside the bucket. I was convinced that this had now all turned crazy.

"Say it! 'Me me me me me.' " Stingo immediately struck side of the bucket with his knuckles making a resounding loud clang.

I thought to myself, "Oh man. He's got a knife…" I could already feel a few tears welling up in my eyes. I was completely mortified.

"Me me me me me!" Stingo reiterated as he hit the side of the bucket again for emphasis.

Terrified, I barely uttered the words, "me me me."

I wanted to go home.

"Louder!"

"me me me."

"Again!"

"Me Me ME!"

"Once more, LOUDER."

I shook as I answered,

"ME ME ME ME ME!!!"

Silence.

Then Stingo took the bucket off my head and set it back down next to the stove. I wiped a few errant tears off of my face.

"That," Stingo stated, "Is your Reptile Brain."

Chapter 7
Mass Insanity

Most people would have given up and never returned after that first baptism by fire. Not me. I kept coming back to the lab. I wanted microscopic vision. I wanted ESP. I wanted genius creativity, just like all those people I saw in the movie that late night on TV.

I wanted to pop my frontal lobes. Whatever that was.

Before long I learned that Stingo's bark was far worse than his bite. The guard dog growl that many people found themselves on the ear receiving end of was just the first thing that separated the men from the boys, the women from the girls. Stingo's sting was his method of testing for the lie. The lie of desiring 100% brain.

Too many just wanted to be entertained for a little bit. Too many wanted a temporary diversion. Stingo had to filter out all of these kinds of people or he would have ended up wasting his whole life on curiosity seekers.

But even if you managed to stick around after the first shock treatment wore off, Stingo was a tough teacher. He would at times appear to be arrogant, unyielding, argumentative, and even crude and corrosive. Then at the drop of a aspen leaf he would transform into the most compassionate, kind, gentle, and caring person you might ever meet.

Stingo often expressed an unusual adult playfulness combined with an unconventional sense of humor that one might expect of a child. His wisdom and experience was housed within a person that might appear as a bellowing sign-waving doomsayer one minute, and then he would be off innocently playing kiddie hide and seek with your brain the next.

To the casual observer it might seem as though he was schizophrenic, a loony bird. But underneath it all, if one looked beyond the surface, one would sense a great depth and wisdom. Ultimately, for the dedicated student, it was the city and all of its inhabitants that seemed insane by comparison.

Stingo lived a relatively simple and carefree existence without all of the trappings of modern life. He lived modestly on a old boot-string budget for necessities and not much more. He was in touch with the core meaning of life that escaped most urban dwellers found endlessly running on the spinning tread wheel of consumerism and materialism. Up at the brain lab, it was you, your brain, and nature. Not much more was required to feel content.

Time with Stingo at the lab, especially if one enrolled for the intensive six-week Brain In Nature course, consisted of an eclectic study of brain physiology and anatomy, behavior science, and psychology. Add to this a dose of mysticism, yoga, and non-denominational mediation. Mix all that with personal counseling, and a measure of plain old sweat inducing physical labor. Top it off with star-lit sing-a-longs 'round the campfire- and you have your Dormant Brain Lab Experience.

I spent the next four years hanging out at the brain lab, visiting every week or so when the weather was nice, and writing long letters to Stingo in the winter when there was too much snow to drive up the narrow dirt road in my Datsun.

Let it be it known, I rarely followed the same standard course of brain self-control prescribed for his regular and paying students, far from it. But I was intensely interested and curious. And I was hard to scare off.

I began to help Stingo with lab chores and assisted organizing and promoting lectures and classes down in Denver. Thus, he tolerated me hanging around and put up with my questions, my stubborn skepticism, independence, and reluctance to follow his prescribed methods to the letter. I expect that he recognized his own rebelliousness in me, and so we got along well enough.

As the years went by, I saw fewer and fewer people at the brain lab. But then, come to think of it, I hardly ever saw anybody up there to begin with.

The 1970's might have been the decade of self-discovery, and that's when the lab flourished. But the decade that followed was that of the Me Me Me Generation. Even though I tried to help Stingo recruit new students, by the time I arrived on the scene starting in 1982, far fewer people were interested in brain self-control beyond a quick sampling, beyond dunking one's toe into the cerebral spinal fluid of knowledge. It seemed like the cultural environment of the 1980's had people focusing on fattening their bank accounts and skimping on their brains.

My circle of friends was a bit different however, and I managed to occasionally recruit my musician and artist buddies to help out for an afternoon. We would gather firewood and drag it down the mountain in exchange for more than a few words of neurological wit and wisdom from the brain man himself.

In time I was absolutely confident that I was on the right track, even though my Big Brain Bang, that internal frontal lobes explosion seem forever illusive.

I had learned to use all kinds of things at the lab that I never expected to master at first- of course, all from their expected and conventional perspective and use: Axes, saws, hammers, but perhaps more importantly pens and typewriters. I also began to look at my guitar a lot differently- after all, Stingo had bought and built the whole lab starting with just three chords and nine folk songs- and his musical axe. Stingo insisted all of these tools were keys that would open up new dimensions for me as well. Eventually.

But first I had to master that amygdala lever, the master click switch in my brain.

*   *   *

Despite my enthusiasm, only one of my best friends took Stingo nearly as seriously as I did. This was a friend of several years, an attractive yoga teacher named Glenda Healthbaar. She was a classic and lithe beauty, of pleasant and unassuming good nature, and she shared the same birthday as myself.

I had met her at the Yoga and Fitness Center in Denver, a place where I had learned and eventually began to teach a few classes myself. She was exactly a year older than me, but unlike me, she had married early in life and already had a couple of small boys to look after. This alone caused her consternation, as both her kids and her husband presented her with unending alarms and challenges, including those concerning her own existence. Thus, she was presented with major impetus to discover how her own brain was put together and reveal what the ultimate purpose of her life was.

Glenda had not bought into the phony for-profit promises of happiness advertised on magazine covers and in TV commercials. She knew meaning was not to be bought in a jar of face cream, a new car, or in a vacation cruise. Stingo and the brain lab offered something unique beyond convention that might bring some order to the inner chaos of her world. She thought he might be able to answer the questions that no one else could, or at least provide some clues so that she could solve these riddles for herself.

One evening after an exceedingly hard all day workout dragging firewood down the mountain trail, Glenda, Stingo and I sat around a small fire collecting our thoughts and resting our bones. The moon began to rise in the darkening sky behind us to the east.

Glenda poked at the crackling flames with a long stick and asked with her distinctively animated and melodious voice, "Stingo, don't you get lonely up here all by yourself most of the time?"

Stingo laughed, "Heck no! I get lonely when I go to the *city*."

Glenda looked at me and remarked, "Uh, that doesn't make sense."

"Think about it," Stingo replied. "Analyze it with your frontals. What IS loneliness?"

Glenda and I looked at each other. I had never seriously contemplated that question before, and I don't think she had either.

"It's when you're all by yourself. When you're not connected to anything, or anybody," she answered.

Stingo smiled broadly and held out his arms widely as if to embrace the forest. At first he said nothing so we could contemplate the answer for ourselves.

Then he offered, "What do you feel up here on the mountain? What do you feel right now?"

Glenda looked around, then closed her eyes and took in a clear deep breath. The stick in her hands dropped to lightly touch the ground. "I feel like I'm part of this. I feel like, like my mind is just another slice of the woods. I feel like you guys are my friends."

Stingo nodded in agreement. "Well, when I'm in the city, I feel like an alien on a strange planet. I can't wait to get home."

Glenda opened her eyes. "Oh! So that's why Niles reminds me of a Martian." She laughed.

I threw a pine cone at her.

Stingo reached over and grabbed a small stick and a rock lying beside him. He held the rock in his right hand and the stick in his left. He began to beat the rock with the stick.

"This rock is the human brain. Your brain. Every day society tries to grind you down, beat you into meaningless dust. Society doesn't know what else to do with this stick except to use it as a weapon, to destroy." Stingo shook his head. "Foolish," he said.

"When you're young, like you are today, you have the strength to resist," he stated as he hit the rock away with the stick. "Use your brain to the fullest. Instead of beating on rocks, you can do other things, creative things..." He tossed the stick in my direction.

Stingo then began to draw a beautiful design in the dirt with his finger, illuminated by the fire. We looked over and saw that he was making one of those yin-yang symbols, surrounded by sun flames. The design flickered with what almost seemed to be a holographic rainbow of colors.

"People make the mistake that they think they're going to live forever. But no one does." Stingo took a deep breath, then looked us directly in the eye, first Glenda, then a slow lingering stare at me. "My dear friends, today is your time. Take charge of it, because if your only here to be entertained, then your not only wasting my time but your time on that precious and fleeting sundial of life."

I looked at the crooked stick that Stingo had tossed and had landed near my feet. I picked it up, half examining it and half thinking about what he had just said.

Maybe it was the light of the fire, maybe it was my head light from exhaustion, but I had a hard time bringing the twig into focus. My eyes watered, and the surface of it seemed to flicker with color like a soap bubble. My mind began to wander.

Everything else around me began to look fuzzy. Stingo and Glenda continued to talk, but they faded away into the background, receding from my awareness and into a twilight dream. I suddenly found myself, inexplicably in what appeared to be a dark space.

I was sitting on wooden planks in the middle of an unlit room. Just a faint ray of sunshine made it's way through a small crack in the ceiling. There were sparkling spots of light, like dim jewels around me, like colored headlights and taillights in the distance.

Suddenly and instantly, everything intensified. I felt and saw sharp bursts of light inside my head like a light show at a Las Vegas showroom. My mind began to race, the light wanting to burst right out of my head. I felt a formless and frightening pain. I'm wasn't sure where I was, here- there- where ever I was- I lifted my hands to the side of my head.

"Niles!" Stingo exclaimed.

Then like a bubble bursting, it was all gone. I snapped out of the trance. I felt Glenda's hand on my shoulder. I dropped the stick.

"You okay?" Glenda asked, her face in front of mine.

Stingo got up and kicked the stick into the bushes with the side of his boot.

"He's okay," Stingo assures her as he sits down and again casually tends the fire with a metal fireplace poker that was stuck into the ground next to him.

I blinked, a little shaken up. "Guess I was exhausted. Worked harder than I thought. Ha." I said.

"Okay now?" Stingo asked me, appearing not overly concerned.

I wasn't sure what happened, but I looked down at my body and it still appeared to be in one piece. I didn't completely expect it to be.

"Yeah. Yeah, I guess so," I replied.

"Traveling can be tough if you're not ready for it," Stingo remarked, poking the fire. "You can get burned."

Stingo looked up at Glenda and myself. He appeared to contemplate revealing something he was keeping to himself. We awaited an explanation.

"The main thing is you've got to master your master gear lever first, your amygdala," he said. He held up the poker. "That's the main thing. Otherwise, you end up places you shouldn't go. It's enough. That's enough for me. Others… I dunno…" He looked doubtful.

Glenda and I looked at each other. Neither one of us knew what was going on. The air seemed like it had been shot through with electricity for a moment, and I was trying to regain my senses.

Stingo looked up at the sky, the stars beginning to emerge. It seemed to have gotten quite dark all of a sudden. His eyes swept across the tops of the trees in the dark forest around us.

He spoke quietly, but intensely, "People don't even see what's in front of their own noses, they don't even see outside the box. I don't know… it's a big universe out there. It's dangerous. You've got to get your own house in order first before you go wandering across the cosmos. It's too easy to get lost."

We sat there wordless for a few more minutes. I was having trouble following him. Finally Glenda broke in, her own chirping voice interrupting the chorus of unseen crickets.

"So Stingo, I've never heard anybody else talk like this, the way you do about the brain. Tell me again how you got interested in all of this brain stuff."

Stingo replied with a wry smile, thinking for a moment. "Okay, come with me." He got up and waved for us to follow.

"Uh oh," I whispered to Glenda. We stood up and watched as he grabbed a flashlight hanging on a hook on the outside of his cabin. He begin to walk up behind his cabin.

"Well, are you coming?" he commanded without looking back. He continued to walk up the hill up to another bigger and longer cabin that sat about twenty yards uphill, the Library.

Glenda and I followed, nothing but the sound of three pair of legs crunching leaves and pebbles under feet as we followed the dim shadow of Stingo behind a wavering flashlight beacon.

Outside the Library cabin hung a hand hewn sign with Cyrillic writing written upon it. Stingo pushed the creaking wooden door open into a dark interior, its contents sporadically lit by the darting dusty beam of the flashlight. We all made our way inside.

We saw Stingo shuffle over to a long workbench where he found a kerosene lamp and matches. He set down the flashlight and lit the lantern. He turned up and adjusted the flame so that the cabin became more illuminated, yet still leaving unlit deep shadows in the corners of the place.

I took a good look around. The place vaguely reminded me of a messy thrift store, a schlock store my mother called that kind of place when I was little.

It was stuffed to the gills with tall file cabinets and large boxes stacked three and four high. There was barely room to navigate the crammed contents. The long wooden work bench and the wall above it had hand tools of all sorts scattered about. Stingo turned around and squeezed between a row of boxes a few feet away, and began to methodically look through a few of them, obviously looking for something specific.

There was a lot of dust and dirt. Glenda coughed and covered her mouth.

"Ah! Here it is." Stingo noted, finding a particular large cardboard box. He picked up the box by the cut-out handles and lifted it up onto the workbench, then turned it end around end so that we could see what he had labeled on its side in big letters:

Mass Insanity

Glenda looked at me, and then at Stingo. "This must have stuff about Niles in it."

I snickered.

"No, no," Stingo replied. "This is what you get when enough people click their amygdala backwards. When you get whole continents of human beans clicking backwards into their reptile brain."

Glenda and I were puzzled.

"War." Stingo explained. "Mass Insanity."

Stingo jiggled the lid of the box free and produced a small plume of dirt and dust that made a small cloud momentarily float in the atmosphere of the kerosene lamp. "Some of my souvenirs from the war," he stated as a matter of fact.

He first pulled out a large ominous looking knife in a leather sheath.

I guess he had this thing about knives.

He unsnapped the sheath and slowly drew out the weapon, holding it up for us to see the ornate decorations on the handle. The blade was thick and serrated and flickered in the reflected light of the lantern. In the center of the handle rested an insignia of a skull and crossbones. Glenda grabbed her throat in fright

"Oh my gosh…" she gasped.

Perhaps it was only a flush of blood through my eyeballs, but I could have sworn I saw the blade flash red for a moment.

Stingo examined the knife himself first, as if to ponder long uncovered memories. "Any tool can be used clicked forward, or clicked backward. A blade can be used to heal or…" he paused.

"It can be used to kill." I finished his sentence. I had learned that lesson. "Precisely."

Stingo handed the knife to Glenda, who reluctantly took it. "My husband has one of these," she said with a drop in her voice.

Stingo raised his eyebrows in surprise.

Glenda continued, seeing his reaction, "Oh! Not one of these! I mean, he's got some knives. But nothing like *this*…"

Stingo went back to digging around in the box, the exact contents just out of our line of sight.

Glenda continued to examine the knife in her hands, and seemed to show some discomfort and concern. Stingo then pulled out some war medals and handed them to me. "This is how you coax boys who haven't even started shaving yet to walk straight into the arms of death. You promise them a medal."

I glanced over at Glenda. Normally she kept her emotions well at bay. But now she was beginning to show real anxiety on her face. I heard her muttering to herself, "…what I'm seeing… this is awful… oh my gosh…"

"What was she seeing inside her brain?" I thought to myself, staring at her with some concern.

Stingo was suddenly aware of Glenda and the anguish on her face. "Here, you better give me that," he said as he quickly but gently took the knife back from her, tucking it back in the box.

There was an awkward uncomfortable silence. Fortunately, this was relieved moments later by the little quick pitter pat of feet on the dirt floor. We all glanced down simultaneously as if on cue and saw a small chipmunk come to a dead stop right in the middle of the three of us. It must have suddenly realized what these three giants were, and scurried off in an instant back under the bench.

"That's the head librarian," Stingo quipped.

Glenda let out a smiling sigh of relief.

Stingo continued to pull out a variety of things, among them a few magazines, a pistol, more badges and medals, his old uniform and cap, and a flag. Stingo had a war story that went with nearly each object. Stingo piled up some of these old things on the bench for us to inspect even as he spoke.

He then took out a conductor's Baton, giving it me. "You like that?" he asked, handing me the stick.

It was just about the last thing I would have expected among a collection of war memorabilia. I looked up at him from the top of my eyes as I examined it and saw he was watching my reaction. "You should know what that is," Stingo said.

"Where'd you get this?" I asked.

"Found it in the basement of a little French chateau dodging bullets one night. It was with some other things. And a book. Must have belonged to a conductor." Stingo pointed his finger in the air and waved it around.

"Oh yeah, it's beautiful," I remarked as I pretended to conduct some music, as I had with other musical batons in conductor class at music school.

I then handed the Baton back to him, and he held it with one hand, and it was as if he was using it to direct his recollections. It was as if he was conducting a symphony of memories that went back far beyond my birth and my world of experience.

Some of his battle stories were too horrendous for me to ever want to repeat in detail to anyone else. War is an ugly affair, and that was the impression Stingo wanted Glenda and I to thoroughly get.

I imagined what it might be like to actually be stuck in the middle of an armed conflict where these things were not just souvenirs, but necessities to survive. I shuddered.

As he explained things, Stingo marched through World War II as an infantry scout for General Patton. He experienced the horrors of war from the front lines. Like my own dad, he had monstrous shells whizzing over his head back in 1945, thinking he might die any second.

We listened to Stingo talk as images flashed through my mind's eye as bright as if they were being projected there in a darkened movie theater. Stingo held up the Baton again, almost as an afterthought while he continued the narration. I began to drift off somewhere else.

I flashed back to an old telegram that my father wrote to his brother during the war. I could see it clearly. I had kept it for years on my dresser never really thinking about what it really meant until I had some of those dusty real bits of war in my hands up on the mountain…

France
Feb. 1, 1945
Pfc. Gene Slade
357 Inf.

Dear Milt,

Don't know why I haven't written you since landing in France except that I thought the letters home would suffice. Now I find that won't do because I must have someone really know how I feel and of course that can't be Mom and Dad.

By the way I'm not in the hospital because I've been hit; damn near wore my left ankle of lugging 42 lbs. of mortar up and down the mountains of Lux. and Belgium before becoming bad enough off to be sent back. In other words I couldn't walk!

Brother dear— be damn glad your ulcers are looking after you! Combat is no place fore man or beast and consequently we turn into a combination that isn't very pretty.

Back here think back over the comparatively few days I've been up front I'm even more frightened over what I have been thru then I was then— and believe me I was plenty shaken then! Up front there isn't much time to think, unfortunately we have plenty here. Incoming artillery is bad but the worst is to have tanks firing at you whether they're coming close or not— their projectiles are so damn fast I wince thinking of them!

My love with kisses to Ida and the baby— God Bless the Russians!

Love Gene

I saw my father's pen in his hand as he wrote the letter. It transformed into a key, and that key had opened a door from his time and place. His handwriting had created the outlines of a hallway that stretched from his world into mine, onto the mountain, up the steps of the Library cabin. I had walked down that hall, transported into his distant world for a moment.

Stingo cleared his throat and brought my attention back. I was safely among the rustling leaves and the sweet and peaceful atmosphere of the mountain. The most dangerous thing I would be dodging would be a falling pine needle.

"Off again, I see. Are you back?" Stingo asked.

"Oh yeah. Sure." I shook my head as I came out of my reverie. "Please go on," I said blinking my eyes.

Stingo smiled at the corners of his mouth, paused for a few seconds, put the Baton back in the box neatly, then went on. "When I got back from the war I asked myself this one haunting question: "Why must I kill my brother?"

"Nobody knew the answer to that one." he continued. "Finally, after ten years and going to three universities trying to find the answer, I asked my professor of neurology at the University of Chicago that question. He told me, 'You're not going to find the answer to that one here in Akademe. If you want to solve *that* riddle, the answer will be in here," as he pointed to his own old gray skull."

"My professor said, 'The answer to why men kill each other in war will be found here, inside the human brain. You can stay here in the university and go slow, or you can go fast and do the research on your own' "

"I wanted to go fast," Stingo said, "So I dropped out of school and started this place. That was thirty years ago." He looked out the cracked window pane above the bench, into the darkness of the forest outside.

Glenda took her finger and wiped off some of the dust on the bench top, nodding her head. "Thirty years since you cleaned, too…"

A long awkward silence.

I looked at Glenda. Glenda looked at me, biting her lip. Then she looked at Stingo, who looked at us both under his bushy eyebrows.

Then we all broke out laughing.

Chapter 8
Thousands of Bugs

After you consciously begin to activate your frontal lobes, you become more sensitive to things we are culturally taught to minimize or ignore completely. Suddenly, clipping your toenails may take on historic significance.

I still hadn't had that highly anticipated Big Brain Bang that Stingo had promised would happen, and I seriously started to wonder if that idea was just a figment of his imagination. But I did start to have what he called "pre-pops". These were sudden and unexpected popping flashbulbs of insight, a brief but enlightening realization, always when least expected. For me, sometimes it happened on the bus. Once it happened while I was flossing my teeth.

These little peak experiences were completely unpredictable. Further, they always seemed to herald a formidable change in life.

Once in a blue moon I got one of these flashes while I was sleeping.

One of Stingo's brain self-control methods, admittedly not a particularly far out or original idea, included keeping written notes of one's dreams for analysis.

Consequently one paid more attention to dreams. This in turn made dreams more intense, which made one pay even more attention to night time excursions, which in turn made dreams even more intense- sort of like scratching a mosquito bite, but in a good way.

Invariably, one would see things in sleep from time to time that inexplicably would show up in life the next day. The first time this happens one can hardly believe it. When it *keeps* happening, one can only guess at what untapped powers await under the cranial mind motor hood.

Every once in a while I had a dream that was so real, so detailed and impressive, that it surpassed the experience of my regular waking life. I couldn't even call it a plain old dream any more. It became more like accessing another dimension

One early morning at about 3 A.M. I had such a totally improbable dream experience in which I was visited by a short one-legged alien with a big head and wide almond shaped eyes that took up half of its head. This creature stood there addressing me on a big undefined foggy plain and gave me instructions:

"Pay attention," the visitor instantly indicated to me, impressing his ideas upon me telepathically with no movement upon the small indentation where it's mouth should have been.

It dictated to me five concepts, all transmitted simultaneously.

Before a moment was even over, my eyelids snapped open in my dimly lit bedroom. I fumbled around on the floor next to my bed and grabbed a pen and a loose piece of paper I kept near me for such an unlikely, but as I had learned, inevitably intense occasion.

Not even bothering to turn on the light, my bedroom lit only by the pinkish sodium vapor street light coming in through my window, I wrote down the message from this inter-dimensional tourist, my nose inches from the slip of scrap paper. Then I collapsed back into normal sleep.

Hours later when I fully awoke the next morning, I lay with my eyes staring at the blank ceiling realizing that I had been approached in the middle of the night. I scoured my brain for details.

There was nothing left to recollect except the vision and realization of the visitation of this extraordinary monopod creature.

Then, I suddenly remembered that I had jotted down his extrasensory dictation.

I turned over and spotted and grabbed the little errant piece of paper lying on the floor next to my bed. I began to read what I had fortunately written down in haste.

I more than expected to become enlightened with something akin to futuristic quantum mechanics or methods of traversing worm holes across vast light years of time and space, perhaps something only Einstein himself could decipher.

But instead of that, the scribble to myself from the alien read these five unexpected blurbs of interstellar wisdom:

Use your heart
Feel joy, appreciate life
Be tolerant of others
Use time well, do your work – wear it like a suit
Don't over desire material – keep material things in their place.

Okay, so it sounded like Mr. Rogers on Pluto.

Another morning, I had another such ultra-vivid dream.

This dream was so spectacularly real it made real life seem absolutely foggy by comparison. Everything was phenomenally alive, everything vibrated with intense importance, I was seeing in a fourth and fifth dimension. It was shocking. It was a real doozy.

I had a flying dream, as was not entirely uncommon for me at least a few times a year. That kind of dream was always memorable. But this one had such astounding colorful clarity and substance to it that it stood apart even from all the other flying dreams of the past.

The manner in which I typically took to the sky in my dream world occurred over and over in a very specific way, and that night's dream was no exception: I was at the brain lab, all alone standing in the small clearing by the water pump. This was near the center of the property just outside the kitchen cabin. I stared at the cabin, and it *vibrated.*

I then gazed up at the clouds, thinking that I would love to see what clouds looked like up close. I held my arms out like they were the cross pieces of a telephone pole and stood up on my toes. With a tiny bit of effort I sprang up into the air and shot above the tree tops.

The feeling as I accelerated from the ground was completely liberating. I could look down and see all of the structures below me and the trails scattered among the trees. I then flew east and skirted over the top of the lab's Eagle's Nest cliff, a four-hundred foot tall wall of rock bordering the east side of the mountain. I flew along the spine of the mountain just inside a ridge. I excitedly began to approach the over ten-thousand foot high summit of Laughing Coyote Mountain.

I could feel the wind in my face and the rays of sunshine on my body. I leaned toward the top of the peak anticipating the glorious unobstructed view that was moments away. I could hardly contain myself, I was certain I would be able to see clear into Utah. I took a big deep breath of exhilaration-

Then suddenly without warning, a microsecond later I was catapulted back into my bed at home in the city.

It had all popped like so much of a soap bubble.

I sat up, completely astonished.

"Incredible…" I stammered to myself. "This must mean *something*."

I knew with certainty that I must drive up to the lab that very day although I didn't know what for. Something was waiting for me.

It was still way too early for me to get up, so I fell back into my pillow and managed another thirty-two winks and snores of a more regular nature. I got up a few hours later, gathered up my things, and after a long drive I found myself at the foot of the brain lab trail. The aspen leaves in the forest were now at their glorious fall peak, a golden hue fit for wallpapering King Tut's dining room.

The air was surprisingly warm at the base trail at 9,500 feet. As I walked up the trail, I had to zip open my jacket as my effort was providing plenty of warmth, even though it was still barely past ten A.M..

I hiked up to the kitchen cabin and stood for several minutes at the clearing. It felt very strange to be standing in the exact place of my dream. I actually put my arms out and stood on my toes hoping that I would take off. Alas, in that morning's real light, my flight was grounded.

I walked over to the kitchen cabin, grabbed the rope and started ringing the bell, "Clang! Clang! Clang!" Those days I deliberately DIDN'T ring ten times, and this was my signal to Stingo that it was me, and not another visitor.

I didn't wait for the "Come On Up!" yell or signal either, because I knew it was coming eventually. If Stingo was too high up on the mountain to hear my ring I would just hike up and find him. I had never come up to the lab and missed him entirely- for some reason, he always knew when he was going to have a visitor.

When I arrived outside the door of Stingo's main place, he was inside on his bed, and completely absorbed writing on one of his old Smith-Corona Typewriters. He looked up and flashed his big wide grin, "Hello Niles! Come in. Come on in!"

I couldn't wait to start telling him about the previous night. "Stingo, I had this dream last night about being here, and it was incredible."

"Okay, okay," he said. "But just wait a minute- let's do this outside." He casually added, "I have something to tell you. I had a feeling you might turn up today…"

He slipped on his old Converse sneakers that had been sitting under the edge of his bed, barely usable and full of holes. I followed him back out the door.

The fact that Stingo claimed that he had a premonition that I would show up completely unannounced, I had no explanation for that whatsoever, except for the fact that his predictions were not completely foreign nor inaccurate.

I began to wonder what his plans were.

"So sit down, sit down, and tell me about this dream," he said as he led me over to the logs outside the door. I then went on to describe my dream in as much detail as I could recall.

Stingo seemed to carefully weigh what I had described. "That's very, very interesting. You know, I tell you to write down your dreams in your journal because they have something you need to know that is escaping your waking consciousness. When you dream, the armor that you carry around with you in waking life is lowered. When we go to bed, we feel safe. When the shields are down this allows cosmic wisdom to filter into your brain. You become aware of things that are normally blocked by self-defense and every day dog-eat-dog, reptile brain survival."

I nodded my head.

"This sounds like a particularly important dream. I'm glad you've come here to follow it up." Stingo stood up and looked down into the valley below.

"Listen," he said turning back to me, "I have to go down to the post office today, and then pick up some supplies way down in Denver. It's going to take me all day, so why don't you just make yourself at home. You can have the whole lab all to yourself."

I enthusiastically replied, "That sounds fantastic!"

He placed a hand upon each knee. "Perfect. Your dream brought you here for a reason. Today, especially."

This was incredible news. Even after all of the years I had been coming up to the lab, Stingo was always there somewhere on the property and I was never completely alone. Although I could always walk all around the hundreds of acres that made up the brain lab, this would be different. I would have the entire mountain to myself.

"If you're here when I get back that's fine, if you're gone, that's fine too. Just enjoy yourself. Do anything you want. Snoop around like a kid. Maybe you'll figure out what the dream meant."

I laughed at the snooping part, but we both knew I'd take him up on it.

Stingo would encourage a certain amount of so-called "naughty behavior" at the lab; Saying anything you wanted to, acting crazy and goofy, getting away with things not considered "proper". It was his way of encouraging students to reject the clutches of cultural conformity and explore forbidden feelings. He didn't mind if you did things you wouldn't dare do at your parent's house.

Stingo went inside to gather a few things for his errand. I just sat on the bench thinking about where I would go and what I would do. Within fifteen minutes Stingo had taken off down the jeep trail and I was left all alone on Laughing Coyote Mountain.

Whoop de do!

I had nearly three-hundred acres of wilderness all to myself, and likely not another soul around for miles. It was beyond exciting!

I decided to first trek up to the very top of Laughing Coyote peak and have a grand view to start the day. Perhaps I would receive a momentous revelation upon the summit, a cracked and steaming halo manifesting around my scruffy dirty haircut.

I left my backpack inside the door of Stingo's place, which he left unlocked as he did every cabin door. Up here, if someone wanted inside, nothing could really keep them out- it would be easy enough to kick a door in or break a window. In the woods, only the skunks would hear you. If Stingo heard you, well, he just didn't run that fast.

I started winding up the trail behind his cabin, and within minutes I was already making efforts to catch my breath upon the steep path.

I didn't mind taking a pause for breath every hundred steps because the scenery in early summer was nothing short of magnificent. The Rockies are a crown jewel of nature. The lab property was a prime example of pristine unspoiled virgin forest, virtually untouched save the occasional hand built log cabin here and there by some near crazy professor of neurology.

I had never actually hiked to the very top of the peak before, although I had come close gathering wood. Usually my trips were always about brain business and little time just spent messing about. But this was a special day, and things would be different. I looked forward to reaching a spectacular panorama about a forty-minute hike ahead of me.

I passed familiar places from previous firewood gathering trips. One spot was just behind the edge of a precipice, and it had a permanent lean-to shelter established there. This spot had been occupied in the past by more adventurous Brain In Nature summer camp participants. On the downside, the wind and weather was quite a bit more robust higher up than it was lower down in the camp among more sheltered woods. On the upside, that campout spot afforded an unsurpassed and unencumbered view, and total solitude.

I paused and took out a small camera from my pocket that I had removed from my backpack before setting out. I set it down on a rock and clicked the self-timer to take a photograph of myself. I continued up the trail.

Unlike Mt. Evanescence twenty miles south, the top of Laughing Coyote Mountain is not at timberline, so there were still plenty of trees to be seen and to wander through.

Finally arriving about fifty yards from the top, I stopped to look at some wild rose bushes because they seemed to look very odd. Something was amiss. From a few yards away, the branches seemed to be moving- or- or was it breathing?! It was completely and unnaturally BIZARRE.

I carefully approached it, and then I suddenly realized what it *was*: The bush was covered in a giant swarm of ladybugs, the likes of which I had never seen before in my life.

There were thousands of them, probably tens of thousands. The branches were absolutely coated with a liquid mass of red and black spotted lady bugs moving up and down like rainbow colored mercury.

At first I was dumbstruck by my observation, and then said out loud to creatures, "Hey! I guess this is my lucky day!"

I sat down in my place and just watched them for a few minutes. The thought occurred that I should get them into my system more directly if I was to benefit from this once in a lifetime experience.

Hmmmm…

I put my hand out next to one of the branches. This didn't seem to faze any of these bugs at all. They were having a party, and my presence didn't have any bearing whatsoever on their gathering, whatever purpose it might have been.

Within seconds they began crawling onto my fingers, then up the back of my hand.

"What the heck," I thought. I let them go up my arm underneath my shirt sleeves.

They crawled over me as naturally as over the native flora. I felt like Saint Frances of the Bugs. In five-hundred years, certainly someone would carve a marble statue commemorating this: A figure covered with thousands of tiny winged warts from head to toe.

"Niles J. Abercrumby, Patron Saint of Natural Garden Insecticides. Pray, and never suffer aphids again."

I sat there for a good five minutes until I began to feel the ticklish sensation of dozens of teeny tiny legs moving around in my armpit. I didn't want to hex my good fortune by accidentally squishing these lucky critters in a sudden uncontrollable urge to scratch, so I stood up and removed my shirt. I carefully brushed off and blew off what must have been several dozen of these quarter-inch organic helicopters. I shook out my shirt, and a small cloud silently flew off into the breeze.

I stood there for a minute and closed my eyes, enjoying the modestly and comfortable breeze flowing across my bare body. I then had what was for me a daring idea, and looked over to the rock outcropping at the very top of the peak that stood moments away.

I jogged over to the rocks, and managed to find the very highest point on the very highest rock at the top of Laughing Coyote Moutain.

There I took off all of my clothes.

I stood there in the light breeze, my arms outstretched, in nothing but my birthday suit for any crow flying by to see and laughingly caw at. "Here I am universe!" I shouted out loud, and slowly began turning around in place.

It was a glorious sensation.

Suddenly I spotted a small dome of tree branches lying about twenty-five feet away. It looked like something made by a beaver who had long lost his way to the pond.

I started on my way off the rock but only got about ten feet- "Ouch! Ow!"

The forest floor was full of sharp little sticks, pine needles, and pebbles. I carefully tiptoed back to the rocks and put my sneakers back on, then returned on my way to the odd pile of branches.

I stooped down and picked up a couple of twigs, examined them, and then glanced down again at the pile. There was something else underneath there, glittering and reflecting the sunlight.

I removed the top layers of branches and found a neatly buried bottle, an emptied ketchup bottle. I picked it up and brushed off the dirt. I saw that inside it were two sticks. This was no beaver at work, but clearly the work of a human.

The two sticks were Chopsticks. With a little effort, I pried off a somewhat rusted cap and shook them out. They showed some sign of weathering, but remained for the most part in good shape, as the bottle had sealed out moisture and weather.

On the surface someone had neatly inked in and colored a geometric lattice of interlaced weaving that gave the impression of basketwork. I thought to myself, "Where have I seen this before?"

It was a very curious find. For a moment I had suspected that they had been left at the top of this peak for someone to use as eating utensils after a long hunger inducing journey. But that didn't seem quite right either. "Hmmmm. Think…"

I then had the sudden urge to jump back upon my perch upon the rocks. I took the two Chopsticks with me and returned to the mound holding one stick in each hand. For no reason whatsoever, like a kid irrationally spinning the wheel on his toy car round and round, I began to spin around like a top, my arms held straight out. I just felt like doing it. Round and round!

I rotated like a symphony conductor who had completely lost all of his wits. I began to laugh at the utter ludicrousness of what I must have looked like if there had been anyone around to see me.

Fortunately it was just me, a few puffy clouds, and of course the company of thousands of bugs close by.

Slowing to a steady rotation, the Chopsticks were my antenna. I was broadcasting a radar beacon far and wide, "Calling all ladybugs! Come to these coordinates!"

In India every twelve years, tens of millions of people gather and cover an entire peninsula for a massive colorful celebration and festival, the Kumbh Mela, a Woodstock on steroids. From a few thousand feet up in the clouds above India, it probably looked the same as the bugs on the bushes looked to me on that day.

For me, all alone with the ladybugs, it was an equally momentous occasion- a spontaneous celebration of being on the mountain, of being alive, and at least for the moment, having all of my worries far away in the city, miles away and far below.

I sung to myself out loud, spontaneously composing nonsensical lyric and melody, my brain humming with euphoria.

"Da dad da a la la loo loooo loooooooooo!"

I counted, and turned around 6120 degrees. That's seventeen complete circles around. Seventeen because my father and I were born on the seventeenth of the month.

Who ever imagined behaving this way? It was all so fantastic-

I declared, "Today I AM Luck. Thousands of bugs- shower me with good fortune!!"

Fortunately, it didn't shower or rain, but was rather a sun shiny day.

However, twirling at exactly 10,042 feet without a stitch of clothing on, no longer perspiring from a strenuous hike, I could only carry on in for about a minute before I started getting goose bumps on every square inch of my body. I was all for a ritualistic baptizing of my own creation, but I didn't see that catching a cold was a necessary part of the experience.

Moments later after I had pulled my clothes back on and grabbed the Chopsticks again in my hand ready to descend, I began to notice something both mysterious, and yet familiar. I first recognized it as the hum that I had heard in my ears the very first day I had visited the lab.

I stood up. "I know what that noise is," I said to myself.

It was just the reverberation of my car engine, I thought.

I held my arms up to stretch, the Chopsticks still grasped in my palms, and the sound became louder.

Surprised, I let my arms fall. Now this was strange. The hum subsided, almost disappearing, but not quite.

At first I thought that it was because the wind might have picked up and the ambient sound of the breeze drowned out the hum. Then I realized, the wind was not even blowing at all, I was standing perfectly still, and I could still hear the noise.

It then occurred to me that I didn't hear the sound earlier because I was busy thinking about something else, or because I was singing.

No matter now, sure enough I raised my arms again, and simultaneously the hum suddenly grew louder.

This didn't make any sense at all. "Do my arm muscles change the way I hear?" I was completely baffled.

I lowered my arms, and the noise decreased again.

An experiment: I raised and lowered my arms a bunch of times, flapping like a crackpot.

So then I started to slowly turn, but this time I paid careful attention to the hum. Sure enough, it got louder still!

I had never realized that my arms had an effect on hearing the sounds inside my own head, much less spinning like a gyroscope, but this certainly appeared to be the case at that moment.

Given all of that, the volume of what I heard in my head was all relative: The sound was not at all loud, even when at its most prominent. It was so faint that the normal volume of a conversation or whistling would be enough to drown out the sensation. But here I was all alone, and I could easily pay attention to something so subtle, and completely focus my attention on it.

I sat down to lace up my shoes, setting the Chopsticks back on the ground. As I was tying my shoes, I realized that the hum had vanished.

"Odd, how odd. That was quick." I thought.

On further reflection I thought that hearing the sound was odd to begin with because I had left my car quite some time ago. It didn't make sense that I would still be hearing engine after-burn inside my inner ear so much later.

But it was equally odd that the sound would quite so suddenly vanish after I had noticed it quite unmistakably just moments before.

I listened very carefully. Nothing. Then I picked up the Chopsticks, and there it was again. I stood up and held the sticks out, and there was the hum again even louder.

I dropped the Chopsticks on the ground and lifted up my hands to cover my ears- so I thought- to intensify the sound by stopping the slight noise of the breeze.

The hum completely disappeared.

"Huh?"

I took my hands away from my ears, heard nothing, then picked up the sticks again. The hum was back, not as loud as before, but it was definitely there. When I spun, the hum intensified again.

It was a very low pitched steady sound like the sound of a great fast and huge turbine behind walls of concrete. It was a presence that seemed to come from every direction, a super low vibration.

I did this several times and came to the inescapable conclusion that this sound was NOT coming from inside my head, but was rather something I was actually hearing from around me, from some part of the environment.

The more I spun, the more I felt as though I was plugging into something completely unknown, and perhaps dangerous. It was beginning to make me nervous. This was not natural at all; This noise was not something I had heard about in my high school geology class.

I turned around in every direction and squinted to see if there was something nearby that could have made the sound. I had an eagle's eye view. There were no manmade structures within sight, nothing like power lines or buildings that could have been the source of the sound.

I suddenly had the notion that I could use the bones in my arms to conduct the sound more directly to my eardrums. So I placed my hands over my ears and then crouched down to place my elbows on the ground.

I sat there with my arms folded and my elbows on the ground, and I must have looked like the rear end of a grasshopper to any of those ladybugs that may have flown nearby. Nothing. It wasn't coming from the ground.

"What is that?!"

Like a scientist who had accidentally stumbled upon some unexplained new phenomenon I remained on top of the peak for a good while more, experimented with the Chopsticks, without the Chopsticks, with my elbows on the ground, with my hands over my ears. Eventually I came to the conclusion that I was absolutely mystified.

None of this made any sense at all. It was thrilling, but it was also extremely unsettling. It started to make me more nervous, very much so.

Stingo had never mentioned such a thing, and I could not even imagine that he would have an explanation. It was becoming as strange as if I had seen a flying saucer in the sky above my backyard in the city.

In the most pessimistic corners of my mind, I began to imagine the Earth cracking apart, that this was the beginning of the end, and that I would soon start seeing eruptions of lava sprout from the ground, or worse. For all I knew, this was signaling the end of the world, mother ships soon to be beaming their invisible destructo rays down upon the planet. I was all alone up here and there would be nobody to grab onto and say goodbye with.

Alright, I wasn't totally convinced that this was the case, but this was definitely disturbing. The euphoria had been replaced by deep concern. A switch had flipped in my brain. I wanted to get out of there.

I quickly went back to the ketchup bottle, replaced the Chopsticks, sealed the cap back on, and buried the Jar under the pile of branches. I was on panicked autopilot now.

I headed back down the trail. What door had been opened? What the heck were those Chopsticks for? Was my dream a subconscious beacon driving me to discover something completely new not only to myself, but to everyone else? Were people down in the city hearing this too?

What had Stingo kept from me? What was I getting myself into?

I felt like I was standing on shifting sand.

Maybe quicksand.

It was time to move to safer ground.

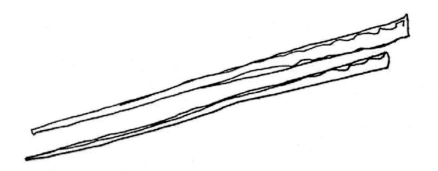

Chapter 9
Deaf and Blind

I began coming down from the top of the trail in rapid descent with this unsettling and illogical hum turning over in my mind. But that lasted only for what was probably only ten minutes, and to no resolve at all. By the time I arrived at Stingo's main cabin the sound was gone, and in more ways than one.

I wasn't at all convinced that my mind was playing tricks on me, not in the least. And *that* was the biggest trick of all: Within sight of Stingo's cabin, I had completely forgotten all of the details of my experience at the top of the peak.

You ask then, "How is it that you report it here now?"

Allow me to explain…

On that day, long ago, my brain had quickly created a safe and comfortable *screen memory* to take the place of an incomprehensible event, the inexplicable low vibration, for which it could not make any sense of.

In this case, my screen memory was the familiar one of the reverberant engine drone in my head after spending time in my car driving, even though *not minutes before I had tested and disproved this possibility*. Rather, my brain completely blocked the real memory of an event because that event was outside all conceivable rationale and logic. It would be years before the true memory would be recovered from a deep crevice within my brain.

This was not the first time such a thing had occurred in my life.

Several years previous I had gotten up one morning in my Denver apartment. I had made some coffee and then ventured out onto my porch.

My porch was a narrow all-weather plastic green carpeted walkway that led down to the front of my building at one end and back to my parking spot behind the building in the opposite direction. Along one side of the walkway was a four-foot high wrought iron hand rail.

On that morning I went onto the porch to look and see what kind of weather the day would bring. I glanced out to find an unexpected surprise in front of me.

It was one of my white sneakers perfectly balanced perpendicularly across the top of the rail.

The first and only thought I had was, "What was my sneaker doing sitting up there?" This made absolutely no sense at all. It was extremely improbable, but that's what I saw. I had absolutely no memory of leaving it there. I couldn't understand who else would have left there either.

But I didn't give it a moment's thought for the entire rest of the day. After all, it was just my shoe. Nothing particularly important about that.

Then, about twelve hours later I suddenly thought of it again. I realized, like finding myself standing in the middle of the street in my underwear, *it had not been my shoe at all.*

At ten o'clock in the evening, the reality of that moment finally unveiled itself to me in a sudden flash of realization.

I remembered that I had walked up to what I initially thought was my sneaker, and then watched it *fly away*, up and away into the blue yonder. And then I completely forgot about it- because THAT JUST DOESN'T HAPPEN.

I didn't think of it again from that moment on until nearly bed time.

It took twelve hours for my brain to make any sense of what I had actually seen-

It had actually been a white peregrine falcon that had perched itself upon the rail.

I had never before seen a peregrine falcon within arms length. Even more so, a falcon had no business being on my porch rail whatsoever. I could not immediately comprehend such a thing. It just did not belong there. I instantly replaced the image of a wild bird of prey on my porch with the closest thing to it in my real daily experience, and that was my sneaker. And I basically forgot about *that* because sneakers don't fly.

For twelve hours, any memory of what I had seen on my porch was totally absent. The peregrine falcon was outside the realm of my experience, and so it did not register. A flying sneaker did not register either.

Only late that evening did it all came back to me. I realized that it was not my sneaker that had flown off into the sky, but a white bird with specific markings on its wing and head that I knew from the cover of a book I had once read, Carlos Casteneda's *Journey to Ixtlan*. The bird was an example of *Falco peregrinus* that was now known to inhabit some of the canyons of downtown Denver. This had been written about in the local paper some month's before. One of the birds had apparently lost its way over to my apartment building and had roosted there for a few moments, at least until I startled it away.

Once my brain subconsciously juggled the pieces properly together, retrieving the details from a long forgotten newspaper article that I had glanced at for a few moments, I actually remembered what I had seen twelve hours earlier. *Yet, almost incomprehensibly, I had completely rejected this scene as it was happening and for a full day afterward.*

This was an astonishing revelation.

Seeing is NOT believing.

I was not able to recognize what I had seen literally right in front of my eyes because the picture was so foreign to me.

Only long later that evening could I finally recall the exact look of the bird's startled gaze, the pattern on its beak, and the marking of the feathers on its body. I had finally recovered from my day long coma.

It has been reported that a hundred years ago and before the entire globe was colonized by modern civilization, primitive island natives looking out to the ocean could not see ships that were as plain as day right on the horizon in front of them. This is said to be because such modern ships were so alien and outside the native experience that even though these people's retinas would certainly have the image of a large sailing ship upon them, the native's brains could not make any sense of this internal optical picture. And so the ships remained utterly invisible to the consciousness of such gazing islanders.

This was the same phenomenon that had prevented me from seeing a rare bird perched on my porch. It just didn't belong there, it did not exist in my experience nor in any of my anticipations, so as it was happening and for ten hours afterward, I could not see it.

In the same manner, it has also been commonly reported that victims of alien abductions substitute familiar and known creatures in place of the memory of the aliens hijacking them aboard their interstellar Winnebagos. The image of an alien being with huge black eyes and small pointy noses is just too far out and too frightening to register, so the abductee replaces the actual image seen with the eyes with a more comprehensible and less threatening face, commonly for example, that of a large barn owl.

Of course, until such abductees undergo therapeutic regression in which they feel safe to remember the actual details of an abduction experience, they have no true memory of such an extraordinary event. Before lying down on a psychologist's leather chaise lounge, they have absolutely no explanation for the group of large owls hovering around them in their bedroom late one night. They have no explanation for accompanying a group of fat birds into their floating silver nest outside. At least not until the therapist tells them "You are getting sleepier and sleepier..."

Then it all comes back with a jolt.

Once as a teenager I had accidentally rode my bicycle at full speed down a hill into a metal road barrier that stood two feet off the ground at the gate of my neighborhood cemetery. I launched myself completely over my handlebars and onto my head upon the hard asphalt road.

By some miracle, like a robot who knew the route, I managed to pedal myself home and walked into the house. My startled mother saw the blood pouring from my head and asked me, "What happened to you?!" I couldn't remember for a full ten minutes. I couldn't even remember what my name was. Eventually, after mom spent some time mopping me up, the memory of what happened filtered back along with a raging headache.

That kind of amnesia sometimes occurs in one way or another when we encounter an incomprehensible mental experience or event. We just don't see it.

As I learned from Stingo, we forget traumatic childhood experiences and adjust our behavior to avoid both the memory of it and of similar painful situations. We subconsciously alter how we live and ultimately our life course-frequently in less than positive ways. We do not remember why. At least not until we make an conscious effort to uncover such things, and then change the way we operate at a deeper level.

And so, my memories of that afternoon alone on Laughing Coyote Mountain was filed away as a hidden file on my brain's hard drive. "That does not compute. That does not concern you. It does not exist."

So, for that moment, on the afternoon upon the mountain by myself, the threat of the unexplainable had been conveniently erased from my mind. Things seemed as regular as ever up at the brain lab once again.

At Stingo's cabin I knew he would not be back for a while and he might not even show up until after I had gone home. So I settled in for further exploration of the lab. This would be a great opportunity to be a real snoop for a change, with little chance of being discovered.

Of course, I knew Stingo really didn't mind me checking out most anything I wished to on the property, as long as I put things back where they came from. I had spent the last few years working as a full partner with Stingo in his efforts to take the lab's findings to the public. On many occasions he had set me off to do whatever I needed to do beyond his immediate watchful eye. Mostly it was just walking around nearby through the forest, collecting firewood, or stepping inside a cabin for a specific chore. I had never done a really systematic survey of the entire place, and this was my chance.

Of course, one might find that among trees and moss there was an infinitely deep story, especially if you were prone to study nature. But that wasn't *my* nature at that time. My attentions were inevitably drawn to manmade things at the lab, at least when I had a chance to poke around.

In this regard, there really wasn't a whole lot that made up the lab to begin with except the cabins and one rickety picnic table for group meals set outside. There was Stingo's main residence cabin with the solar window wall, the printing cabin, the kitchen cabin, the bath cabin, the library archive cabin. Then there was a remote guest cabin that saw very little use, none really that I ever knew of.

There were a couple of very small structures built into the hill or ground that housed supplies, and a couple of those rudimentary lean-to shelters for Brain In Nature participants.

No matter, this was my chance to really examine the property at my leisure in any detail, and I immediately set out to work to make the rounds. One of the first places I did poke around was in Stingo's main residence, the one with the solar window wall where he stayed and slept most of the time.

This was perhaps the most interesting place, jammed packed with a thousand books, knick-knacks, writing and printing equipment, photos and magazines, and file cabinets crammed with reports and papers. I started going all around all the place, hardly knowing what to pick up next.

I climbed up onto the bunk using the stove as a step stool, and found the guitar case and a banjo case which I had spotted on my very first visit. The ornate label on the edge of the platform written in Stingo's odd Cyrillic code was still there. It still looked Greek to me.

Inside the case was an old guitar. It was not the cheap one that I had seen Stingo had play on the Groucho Marx show, but rather a Martin D-28, a beautiful and exceedingly valuable instrument that I later learned was built in 1958. This was clearly a fancy guitar Stingo had treated himself to after he achieved a certain amount of fame and fortune.

Stingo had written something in Russian with a bold magic marker (of course) in the bottom corner on the top of the guitar, personalizing it in this way. I strummed a few chords and noticed that the neck had warped a bit and that the strings were high. The guitar would need some luthier work to play properly again.

Next to it was another case containing an old Vega banjo. I strummed that as well. For me, a banjo was as impossible to play as some Chinese yueqin, so I didn't bother with it much.

I put them both back carefully and climbed down.

I turned around and contemplated the scene in front of my eyes, something that I had really not paid too much attention to before. His stove was disgusting.

It was covered with dirt and bits of food. I lifted the lid on a saucepan and to my astonishment found an uneaten piece of meat. I think it was the remnants of a steak.

This was a big surprise to me because Stingo had always advertised nothing but healthy vegetarian meals for the summer brain camp. Was he sneaking cooked ground cow to himself on the side? Okay, I wouldn't hold him to it.

But besides this, I don't think his stove had been cleaned in ages upon ages. There was dirt that had dirt on top of it. You could have written a copy of The United States Constitution with ink made from all of the grease on that stove. Good lord, it was horrible.

I grimaced.

Questions about whether or not the health department would declare his wood stove a health hazard would have to be answered at some other time. I had far more interesting things to look at for the time being.

I spent a good couple of hours walking around. I visited every spot in the brain lab. I found it extremely interesting, not at all typical of a vacation spot or summer cabin that some family would visit on the weekends. Every corner contained riddles in the manner of objects that I didn't understand. Everywhere were Stingo's cryptic notes to himself pinned to the walls or on the walls themselves, as well as cabin wall graffiti from scores of past lab visitors and Brain In Nature participants.

And then there were the tree objects.

Everywhere you walked on the property things were scattered in the trees. By this, I don't mean objects were just thrown up into the canopy of flora, but rather that the trees branches had actually grown through these things. The things were impossible to remove unless you broke them or broke a branch. The clear evidence was that people had deliberately sewn small branches through objects years ago, and the tree branches had long since thickly grown around or through the items.

On one tree there was a roller skate, and the tree's branch had grown through the openings in the portion that held your foot in place. That firmly and permanently adhered the skate to the tree as if the tree were preparing to roller skate down the mountain.

There were Bottles and Jars in the middle of branches, sometimes where a hole had been drilled through the bottom of the glass and the tree branch wore the bottle like a bracelet.

Other trees held other old children's toys. There was a toy tennis racket being worn by one aspen like a necklace. There was a bicycle wheel with the spokes removed, and a pine tree wore it around the trunk like a collar. Another tree wore an old pair of glasses, on one side the lens still in place and a branch woven through the other side, the lens long gone.

Other trees held old rusty tools and gave the impression that the tree had long ago used the tool, now claiming the tool exclusively as its own.

Then there were the metal tags, little aluminum tags found all over the property. These were made with some kind of tool like a rotary stamp that embossed the lettering on a strip of metal. One dead tree truck over by the main water pump had one of these labels that quite appropriately said "Entropy Is Entropy".

Typically these embossed messages were a puzzle, a koan that you could ponder the meaning of for quite some time and never come to any definitive conclusion.

I continued to go around one by one, and visited all of the cabins. I saved the remote guest cabin for last. This was a place I had only seen from the outside on one other occasion. It was located far away from the rest of the structures, all of which were centrally located on the property.

I walked the foot trail towards the cabin until the path ultimately faded away completely, giving testimony to the lack of visitation to this spot. I continued to walk in the same general direction and finally caught a glimpse of it through the aspen tree trunks.

The look of aspen trees always interested me because the trunks are covered with what looks like *eyes*. As I walked among them, I always had this peculiar feeling that I was being watched by the trees and the spirits within them.

I arrived a dozen yards in front of the building. The guest cabin sat at the edge of a beautiful meadow with a weather beaten rocking chair sitting on its small narrow wooden porch. I stood for a moment and paused to take it all in. I almost felt as thought I sensed a special kind of energy emanate from the peak of its roof. Certainly my imagination.

There were two small quant attic windows right in the corner under the roof apex, and each one had a red frame around it just like in a storybook gingerbread house.

As I walked up to it, I wondered why I had never taken the time to spend time here before, as it was such an idyllic setting. I certainly had never be encouraged by Stingo to do so. In fact, I couldn't ever recall him even mentioning the place. *I couldn't remember how I even knew about it.*

Maybe I had just stumbled upon it wandering around previous. It was quite odd and a conundrum. Certainly, it never came up in conversation.

Ah well, no bother.

The air was absolutely fresh and clean. A very slight breeze moved the grass and wildflowers in front of me. There were deep red Indian Paintbrush by the thousands covering the football field sized slope that began at the wooden stairs at the foot of the cabin.

I walked up the two creaky wooden steps and sat down in the rocking chair, slowly rocking and listening. It was very peaceful and calm, both outside as well as inside my head.

After a few minutes I decided to get up and investigate inside. I pushed the door open and entered.

The interior of the cabin was very simple and plain: A small cot by one wall, a small wooden desk with an kerosene lamp under the window, a shelf that contained a single cup, a couple of plates, and a few pieces of cheap silverware. There was a small wood stove in the corner with couple of pieces of wood next to it.

Unlike all of the other cabins at the brain lab, this one lacked the abundant graffiti on the walls as well as the common plethora of tools and knick-knacks everywhere. This gave some evidence that people rarely came to the place. And so it looked like exactly one might expect a modest vacation mountain cabin to look like on the inside.

Inside there was a wooden step ladder, a primitive staircase leading to the sealed attic. Although all of the other cabins were a single room, this small cabin had a separate attic above the ceiling rafters, closed off from the main floor.

I began climbing the small ladder to the attic door, which was nothing more than a flap in the ceiling. After six steps up I looked to find that the flap had a small keyed padlock on it.

"Hmm, that's unusual," I thought to myself. I couldn't think of a single place on the lab that Stingo locked up. This was for practical reasons more than anything. If a trespasser wanted to steal something, it would take nothing to kick in a door or break a window, so better to let people poke around and finally realize there was little of monetary value on the property. As for the students and subjects spending time on the mountain, there were little secrets, certainly nothing involving physical items.

Although I was very curious as to the contents of the attic, I certainly wasn't going to commit breaking and entering, so I descended the ladder back down to the floor.

It was a little stuffy inside, and so I decided to open the window. With a little effort I managed to slide it up, although it was quite resistant. For all I knew, it might have been years since anyone had actually let some fresh air into the place.

I went over to the small bed and proceeded to brush off the dust and a dead spider. There was an old Gilpin County Newspaper on one end of the bed. I sat down and began to read, "Casino Life For County's Future?" The article was about the dreary economic reality for Gilpin County, seat of the brain lab.

Gilpin County had one small town of historic note, a tourist destination by the name Central City, home of the Colorado Gold Rush in the late 19th Century. It came to be called "The Richest Square Mile On Earth" from all of the gold mines in the area. A hundred years later however, Central City was falling apart, and might have now been renamed, "The Tackiest Square Mile On Earth".

The only remaining and opened businesses was a seldom visited art gallery, a little run down grocery store at the edge of town with a post office counter in the back, and a few shops crammed full of "Authentic Colorado" tourist souvenirs (made in China). And even at that, the tourist trade had dwindled considerably.

So it was that Gilpin County officials were planning a Colorado ballot proposal that would legalize gambling in Central City and neighboring Blackhawk, and raise enough local revenue to save the community from total extinction.

I suddenly realized how utterly exhausted I was. I couldn't think another thought. I collapsed back down into the creaky squeaky bed.

Lying down on my back and quickly scanning the newspaper article I had no idea of the future consequences of legalized gambling on the very existence of the brain lab and the survival of this unspoiled patch of Mother Nature. I began to drift off into a wonderfully pleasant slumber on the bed with the sound of a gentle breeze coming through the window.

Chapter 10
Brain Radar

I was on a swing, silently flying back and forth, looking past my legs and watching the ground scoot past me, first in one direction then the other. My feet were extended straight out in front of my blue tennis shoes like the nose cone of a rocket.

I was getting ready to launch myself off of the seat as I had countless times before as a kid. Suddenly I heard the sound of the old school bell, "clang clang clang", and thought to myself, "Oh man, recess is over already?! I'm just starting to have fun!"

Wait a second, my school didn't have *that* kind of bell.

Then I opened my eyes. I wasn't in the school yard at all, and the bell I had been hearing wasn't an modern electric school bell, but rather the bell on top of the kitchen cabin at the brain lab. I had been dreaming.

I sat up and thought, "Who's that?" listening carefully. But the bell had now stopped. I got up, left the cabin, closed the door behind me, and started off in the direction of the main part of the lab property. It was starting to get dark out, and I knew that I had better hurry as it would be too easy to get lost off of the main trail.

I looked up and realized that I must have been asleep for at least a couple of hours. The sun had vanished and was not visible between any crack of treetop limbs. I had lost track of time. Whether or not I remembered all of the details of my hike to the top of the peak, around all the cabins and property, then falling asleep in the guest cabin- it had taken up the whole day.

I came to the kitchen cabin and looked around in the dim light. Nobody there. Then I saw that Stingo's jeep was back. Placing my hand on the warm engine hood I knew it must have been him ringing the bell to announce his arrival back home. I started up the trail back to Stingo's place and shortly stood at his red door and saw him inside unloading some grocery sacks. He had lit a couple of lamps that stood on the filing cabinet. The cabin was filled with a subtle flickering yellow light that cast a few dancing shadows on the log walls and on the books upon the shelves.

"Hey Stingo," I said knocking then pushing open the door.

"Niles, my good man, come on in. How was your day?" he replied.

"Fantastic- I walked around everywhere, snooped around." I searched my mind, which strangely came up a bit blank. "I can't even remember everything, actually…Haha."

I scratched my head.

"Good, good. Find anything interesting?" he asked nonchalantly, preoccupied with his shopping bounty, counting to himself a survey of all of the goods he had set out from the bag.

"Oh gosh, yeah…" I said haltingly, trying to remember the details of the day, but drawing nothing but a fuzzy approximation. "Saw a million ladybugs… and what else… um…" I shrugged my shoulders.

Stingo walked over and grabbed the stool from the corner without saying anything. I knew to sit down. He then plopped down on the bed which I then noticed had a large pile of unopened envelopes on it of all sizes and colors.

Stingo took his hand and then spread out the envelopes so they nearly covered a square yard on his bed. Then he just sat there and gazed at them.

I immediately forgot about myself and noted Stingo's strange behavior. "What are you doing?" I asked quizzically.

"I'm figuring out which ones to open first," he replied. "I get so much mail, it's easy to open up the wrong letter and have a good consciousness flow wrecked."

I tilted my head to the side because I didn't quite understand why it would matter which letter you opened first when you got your mail. "What difference does it make?" I asked him.

Stingo looked me in the eye. "Do I ever leave my cabin door wide open?"

"No, I don't think so," I said.

"Why not?"

I sat there and thought about it for a few seconds. "Because you don't want the flies to come in?"

"That's only part of the reason," Stingo answered. He looked at me and tapped his finger tips together gently. I knew he wanted me to think about it some more.

I sat for a good thirty seconds and scratched my head, again. "I dunno, I give up."

"It's to keep the squirrel brains out."

Stingo sat there, still looking at me. I knew this was some sort of lesson.

"Yeah, okay…" I said, hoping he would fill in the completely blank slate that was my mind at that moment.

"If I just leave the door open, the squirrels come in, and they wreck the place. They tear everything apart looking for nuts. Next thing you know all my papers are all over the place."

I slowly nodded my head. I've seen how squirrels have shredded the seat cushions on my mother's back yard chairs. And I've seen how they have delighted in absolutely torturing and teasing her dogs from the trees and fence top. My ex-girlfriend Sarah once called squirrels "Nothing but rats with furry tails." This seemed a bit extreme, but might have been fairly accurate according to taxonomy. I hope she hadn't be referring to me.

Stingo continued, "I like to keep my brain nice and tidy. Peaceful. When I get a letter from a person whose brain is complete chaos- you know, not much more brain power than a rodent looking for peanuts- I have to be ready for it, otherwise it's like a squirrel coming into my cabin and creating a complete mess."

"Ah ha." I understood.

Stingo turned to one of the shelves behind his bed and started rummaging through a open Jar that contained a jumble of Pens. He selected an old fancy maroon fountain Pen, removed the cap, and then loosely held it in his left hand. He then turned back to the letters and waved both of his hands over the letters on his bed, his right palm open and facing down. He halted this process then looked and spoke to me to explain.

"To know which letters are safe to open first, I use my *Brain Radar*. The ones that are filled with a lot of entropy I put away for last. I make sure I'm good and ready for 'em."

Stingo turned back to the assortment of mail and closed his eyes tight, pointing his nose up in the air melodramatically. He shuffled the letters one more time.

He began to pour over the letters, slowly passing both hands over them all. His hands moved back and forth for a few moments like the white plastic pointer from a Ouija board. I saw the loose fountain pen bob and dip a little, but I was fairly certain that this was just because how he was holding it.

For a moment I envisioned somebody using a dowsing rod to find water. As a kid I had played with forked tree branches in that manner, but of course my parents wouldn't have approved of me digging up the back yard to find an underground stream to verify my hunches. Besides, all of our faucets worked perfectly well. (Note the pun.)

Stingo cocked his head to the side as if he was hearing something. I certainly couldn't hear anything, the cabin was dead silent. Eventually he slowed and settled over one plain manila envelope, secured with multiple layers of tape.

He suddenly darted down and plucked up the envelope. He opened his eyes, and turned to me, "This one!" he exclaimed, and then carefully used the pen to mark three neat plus signs and an exclamation mark in a row on the top of it. He then handed it to me. "You open it."

I hesitated for a second then took the envelope from his hand and worked it open, engaging my teeth to do so. I then removed the tightly folded stationary inside and tossed the empty envelope back on the bed. Stingo urged me, "Go on, open it up."

I unfolded the letter and something green slid out to the floor like leaves dropping off of a tree. I looked down to see what had fallen out. My mouth fell open as I bent down to pick them up: Three crisp new $100 dollar bills.

I showed Stingo the money and handed it to him. He quietly folded the money into his shirt pocket. "Go ahead and read it," he instructed.

"Dearest D.A.," I read. "Thanks for all of the encouragement two months ago regarding the film offer. As you suggested I took the opportunity and it was to my distinct advantage. I hope this will in some way compensate you for what has been continuing support and good guidance over many years. My best to you, Anthony."

Stingo was looking at the return address as I read. As I finished, he pointed to it and said, "Anthony Zerba. Hollywood. He's an actor."

Stingo gathered up the remaining envelopes into a pile. "I'll look at the rest later. That was the best one of the lot."

My first thought was that this was a pretty amazing demonstration, picking out an envelope among a large pile, more or less blindfolded, to find one of such importance, not to mention cold hard cash.

He gathered up all of the letters and rose from the bed, starting towards one of the file cabinets.

Then my second thought was, "Wait a second- was this a trick? Some clever slight-of-hand?"

At that thought Stingo turned and looked straight at me and squinted at me. I hadn't said anything out loud. "Hold on a second…" he uttered.

Stingo threw the letters all back down on his bed again including the empty one that I had just opened. He tossed the loose pile like a little kid playing with a pile of leaves, then spoke.

"Energy flows in two directions, actually it flows in all directions. But for our purposes here, I'm trying to pick up on the positive energy stored in these envelopes."

Stingo grabbed my arm and said, "Switch places with me." He got up and gestured me to sit on his bed in his place as he moved over to the stool.

"You know how you use Healing Hands'?" he asked. He was referring the practice in which one clicked into increased frontal lobes sensitivity and then uses the hands to "comb" entropy out of another person to promote healing.

This was a basic brain lab exercise that novices learned fairly early on. In this brain exercise, one student would lie down and completely relax while another would perform non-touching motions, moving the hands slowly over the "patient's" body, as if one were brushing the hair on a pet dog or cat. Anyone watching this would think it was total insanity or fake mumbo jumbo voodoo. But the fact was, it was very easy to detect some kind of subtle energy movement during this practice.

Nutty as it might seem to some, this Healing Hands practice eventually was corroborated as a factual and legitimate method of reducing the healing time for wounds in at least one serious legitimate double blind laboratory experiment. Years later when I was researching numerous claims Stingo had made decades earlier, I had read about such techniques in a periodical published by ISSEEM, The International Society for the Study of Subtle Energies and Energy Medicine.

"Here, take this," he said as he put the fountain pen in my left hand and closed my fingers around it. "Don't hold the pen too tight, you'll cut off the flow. You'll also get ink all over everything."

His hands felt unusually warm. It immediately reminded me of the mother of one of my students, Muffy Dornknob. Once after we had been talking about biofeedback, she showed me that she was able to consciously raise the temperature of her hands simply by concentrating on them. It was so quick and startling that I could see her hands turn beet red right in front of my eyes. They felt just like they had been under running hot water.

"I use the Pen as an antenna, but don't concentrate on it too much. It's your brain that has to amplify the raw signal. Hold your hands like this over the letters," Stingo said as he moved my hands in a clockwise flat rotating motion. "Close your eyes and see if you can sense a feeling of expanding warmth." This was actually the first time he indicated to me that an ordinary looking object could be used to do something extraordinary.

I shut my eyes and slowly moved my hands as he instructed. I felt nothing. "I dunno," I said. "I can imagine what you are saying, but…"

"That's fine," Stingo replied. "That's a start, just go with that, that's your frontal lobes starting to kick in, your imagination circuits. Just go with that for now. The Brain Radar will bleep in on its own without you forcing it to."

He let go while I continued for another minute. I then began to feel a distinct feeling in my hands, a pleasant tingling, a sensation of warmth, a kind of gentle magnetism.

He elaborated further, "The Pen is like a fishing pole, and you're trolling for a bite. Feel for a little bobbing, that's all. You're not spearing a whale."

Then Stingo spoke in a softer voice, "When you start to get something, follow it, let it draw your hands down, don't force anything. You follow IT, not the other way around. And it's not a race, take your time."

I continued to move my hands, and within a couple of minutes I felt as though I could sense a number of almost imperceptible vortexes on the bed sheet, like little warm jets of current moving up from below my hands. The current actually felt like it was drawn to the Pen and then radiated to the other hand, then up through my arms and into the rest of my body. It was a remarkable, yet very subtle sensation. If I had a bad itch, which I didn't, I would have missed it.

I opened my eyes a crack to see if it was actually vibrating, but to my surprise I really couldn't see anything physical at all.

"Try again," Stingo urged. "And no cheating this time."

He took his hand and brushed my eyes closed. With my eyelids sealed I could hear Stingo noisily reshuffling the letters on his bed.

"Find the warmest one, the strongest one, and move towards it..." Stingo seemed to know exactly what I was feeling. I then kept my eyes tightly shut and was closing in on something with both hands, about a foot above the bed.

"Go for it!" Stingo suddenly urged, and I quickly plopped my hands straight down onto an envelope. I opened my eyes and lifted up the letter. It was the very same envelope from Zerba that had contained the thank you note and the money.

Stingo smiled broadly and nodded his head, then patted me on the back. "Impressive," he complimented me.

He took the envelope from my hand. "That was amazing," I remarked. "How is that possible? I mean, the money's not even in there any more."

"Simple," Stingo said. "You know how when you rub a balloon against your shirt you add a charge to it, static electricity makes it stick to a wall?"

"Sure."

"Whenever you do something, your energy and your intent infuses the objects you touch with that same energy, for a while at least. If you have positive survival enhancing intent and energy, it's stored in the things you touch at that moment, like a battery. It stays there until something discharges it, or reverses the charge."

"I see," I said, thinking about the stack of rechargeable batteries I kept in my kitchen drawer at home.

Stingo pointed to an empty Mason jar with a screw-on cap sitting on the bookshelf nearby. "If you knew how, you could store positive energy in that Jar over there, just like a piggy bank."

He arched his eyebrows in a comic motion, just like Groucho Marx in one of his comedies. "Was he serious?" I thought.

Stingo went on, "When you approach such an object with a positive charge, it feels like something growing, like a seedling coming out in the sun."

"Oh yeah!" I blurted out. "I know, when I charge up one of my batteries in my recharger, it gets warm, sometimes even hot to touch."

"Exactly. In the same way, if a person is clicked backwards into their reptile brain and computing "me me me", then they infuse an object with negative *entropy*. If you train yourself to be sensitive to these forces, when you get near such an object you'll feel like you're peering over a chasm, like you're going to get sucked down the toilet bowl." Stingo motioned his hand like he was pulling a chain, "Whooooosh, down the drain into the sewer."

I laughed.

"Everybody does this to things whether they know it or not," he said. "But hardly anybody can sense these charges. It can be done here in wilderness without too much effort. Down in the city there's so much interference it's harder."

He pointed to the pile of letters. "Now do it again. This time feel for a hole, a void, move your hands in the opposite direction, counter clockwise, counter intuitive and against the grain. Your brain is like a radio receiver, you can tune into any station you want."

I closed my eyes again and held my palms above the letters as before. It was easier to sense the subtle but distinct feeling of energy rising up from the bed, but this disappeared quickly as I reversed the motion of my arms. I moved my hands for about twenty seconds, and then finally I felt something different.

"Hey, there's a couple of cold spots," I remarked. I hovered above one and it sent a shiver up my spine.

"Precisely," Stingo answered. "Find a good popsicle."

There were a few luke-cold creamsicles, but there was one definite subzero icicle that I focused on. It made a prickly needle sensation on my right hand and felt like someone stuck a frozen thorn there "Yuck!" I said as I instinctually scratched the bottom of my right hand for relief, like a dog with a flea bite. Without thinking about it too much, I again plopped my hand down and opened my eyes.

I saw that my hand was on top of a couple of letters, but I knew the one I wanted was on the bottom. I dug down and plucked it up, then held it up like the winner of an Academy Award for Worst Movie of The Year. "This one!" I exclaimed.

Stingo took the letter from me and looked at it. He slowly nodded his head in recognition. "Perfectly done," he said.

He turned the letter around for me and pointed at the return address. I read it, and although the address didn't ring a bell, the initials did. It said, "L.B." I knew who had sent this letter and I had heard more than one story about the guy who left his paw print there. Lyin' Badmouth was his name.

"Bulls-eye." Stingo held out his hand for me to shake in congratulations, then he looked back at the letter. "I won't get fooled again, no sir-ree. Give people the benefit of the doubt, but not twice. You ever seen one of those angler fish?" Stingo wiggled his finger in front of my nose.

I knew what he was talking about, a fish that sits on the bottom of the ocean that has a long appendage attached in front of its big mouth to lure its prey.

"Here's a nice big juicy worm for your dinner, yum yum yum…" Then Stingo opened up his hand like a jaw and instantly clenched it tight. "Then GULP!!! You just became a nice meal."

Stingo smiled again. "The smiling predators are the worst kind. Wonder what he's offering this time, wonder what he wants? Probably the deed to the brain lab in exchange for a few hours work."

Stingo gathered up all the letters off the bed. "This one goes to the bottom of the pile. Got to be very careful." He went over to one of the metal filing cabinets, slid open a drawer and deposited the remaining letters into a folder. He shut the file drawer with a metallic clank. Then he turned back to me. "I want to show you something."

Stingo stepped over to the foot of his bed and kneeled down. For a second it looked like he was going to fold his hands and start saying a bedtime prayer. But I figured that such a thing wasn't very likely.

He looked up at me and said, "You never know when an emergency comes along. You can be a grasshopper, or you can be a smart ant," he said.

I felt the top of my head for antenna sticking out, thinking briefly of the famous Aesop's tale.

"If there's ever an emergency, you should be prepared. I know I can count on you to help me if it comes to that, so I want to show you something that you might need to know about, or maybe not."

Right at the foot of his bed he started messing with the stone foundation that he had built under the base of his box spring. It consisted of an assortment of irregular flagstones all about the size of a book, all mortared together with rough cement.

I had always looked at it and thought it was a nice decoration. Suddenly he grasped a section of the rocks and he pulled out a couple of long, flat stones. These two weren't cemented in place, but were only held in place by the sheer friction of stone against stone.

Stingo stuck his hands inside the dark hole and with some effort began to slide out a large gray metal tray. The handle appeared to be made from what was probably a bent piece of wire clothes hanger.

It looked like a safe deposit drawer. It was about a foot across, maybe two feet long and a few inches deep. It took quite a bit of effort for him to move it out completely onto the floor. It made a scraping noise against the flagstones on the floor as he did this. Obviously it contained something of considerable weight.

He unlatched and then swung open the lid. I gasped.

The entire box was stuffed full with large shiny metal coins, rows and rows of them.

Stingo pried a couple of them out and handed me one.

"Here, you can have one now, take it." He said.

"Have one?" I asked unbelievingly. I held the coin up to my face and carefully inspected it. It was a 1921 silver dollar. I turned it around in my hand. "Wow, thanks, but you don't have to," I said, still in awe glancing down at the treasure chest that lay in front of me.

"No, take it. Money doesn't matter to me except to buy things I need to survive and things for work, Stamps and paper," Stingo said. "Just keep it as a token of friendship and trust."

"Thanks D.A..," I replied. "Wow, thanks."

Stingo removed the money from his shirt pocket and neatly tucked the hundred dollar bills into the drawer. "Now, you're to keep this drawer a complete secret to yourself. I've only told a couple of other old staff about this, and that was years ago. They're long gone doing their own thing. I don't expect them to come around much and I can't count on them in an emergency."

Stingo closed the lid and began to move it back under the bed. I helped him because it was harder to put back than it was to slide out. Stingo carefully fit the granite slabs back in place.

Stingo didn't stand up nearly as easily as he had kneeled down. He had to lean on the bed, and pushed himself up with his hand on one of his knees.

"What do you mean, what kind of emergency?" I asked.

Stingo sat down on the bed. "When I started this place I was young. That was almost thirty years ago. I've been very lucky, but you never know what is around the corner."

I was wondering if he knew something I didn't.

"Your Brain Radar will keep you out of harms way most of the time, but sometimes you'll get distracted. You need redundancy backup. Always have backup."

He brushed some dirt off his blue jeans and continued. "An emergency. You don't know. You can predict what will happen half of the time. The other half of life is a complete surprise. Predictably chaos."

For some reason I had long misinterpreted Stingo and his work to imply that brain self-control meant that as you learned to control your brain, you eventually controlled everything that happened to you. I naively thought that becoming Master of Your Own Brain was equivalent to becoming Master of the Universe; that eventually you learned to manipulate the universe so that only "good" things happened in your life.

Stingo walked over to the wide window panes that made up the entire south wall of his cabin and looked outside and up towards the sky.

"The universe is half light and half dark. Half of the time it's light outside, but the other half of the time it's night, and the sun is hiding. Some times it's spring and the flowers are popping up. Other times it's fall and things are dying. You can't change that." He gestured with his arm and hand to motion like leaves falling.

I looked outside and saw the wind blow and scatter some leaves which fell from the aspen trees just yards away. The falling leaves illustrated his point, perfectly in sync with his statement. It was like magic, like he brushed the leaves off of the trees by waving his hand. Of course, I consciously dismissed the notion as quickly as it occurred to me. Such a thing seemed preposterous to me at that moment. I never thought of him as Merlin.

"Winter lasts from September until May around here. The trees are bare half of the time. That's how life is too. Easy times come and go. I used to make $2000 an hour on TV, and now I don't make squat. But I manage with squat- using my brain." He tapped the side of his head.

I laughed with the way he delighted in juggling words. "But you're happy, right?" I asked.

"Sure, of course! I don't need a lot of money, it just gets in the way." Stingo smiled as he nodded his head enthusiastically. "I wouldn't have it any other way. Using your brain means that you recognize how the pendulum swings. Sometimes you're rich, and sometimes you're poor. Sometimes things are easy, and sometimes things are hard as hell. When you tickle your amygdala and use your frontal lobes, it means you know how to surf the waves, and how to keep the inside of your head from turning into mashed potatoes. It doesn't mean you can avoid the white water entirely."

I thought of a few people who had instant potatoes where their brains used to be. I could see them now, applying salt and butter to their ears.

"If you land hard on your rear end too much, life is no fun. The game is to land with your feet on the ground, and that's a tricky business no matter what. If you can stay on your feet most of the time, life is a lot more fun. WAY more fun. You gotta' be a Cosmic Surfer."

Stingo did a funny little pantomime of a surfer keeping his balance, arms straight out to his sides.

"You have to wrestle with your own humanity, and with the rest of humanity. Unless of course you want to live in a cave. Then life's easy, then you don't have to worry about anyone, not even the barber." Stingo combed his hand through his hair, exaggerating the motion.

"You got a hair cut today!" I exclaimed. I hadn't even noticed it until that moment.

"*No.* I didn't get a hair cut," he said dead seriously. "I got thousands of them cut, probably ten thousand! Was wondering if you would notice… Haha!" he laughed.

Stingo typically let his hair grow long, often nearly down to his collar and sometimes even longer. But now he looked as neat as a school teacher. Well, a teacher at an alternative school anyway.

He then abruptly continued his previous line of thought and looked me square in the eye. "Some things you leave to chance, but the important things you control as best you can. Some things are too important to gamble. But gamble, that's what people do, every day."

I stepped back and folded my arms to contemplate all of these things he was saying. And then I stepped right back into the tree trunk that held the roof up in the middle of the cabin. "*OW!*" I had knocked my head into the short knub that remained from of one of the sawn off branches.

"Hey, be careful when you're walking backwards," Stingo suggested as he examined the back of my head. "No blood, you're okay."

I rubbed my head.

"You see this tree trunk here?" he asked.

"Yeah, sure." I turned and looked up and down the bare and shiny trunk, of course covered with typical brain lab graffiti.

"Didja ever look at this?" Stingo said as he examined the writing up the trunk, gliding his hand down the surface.

I turned around and started examining the smooth tree trunk. It was funny, I had looked, but I hadn't really SEEN what I had looked at before. I looked carefully this time. It consisted of nothing but names:

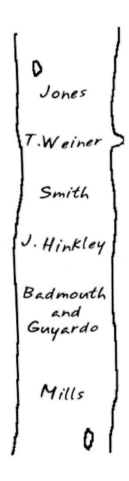

There were over a dozen in all.

"See the names here?" he asked. "These are people- brain lab flunkies, drop-outs that never transcended into their frontal lobes. They thought that clicking their amygdala forward was a big joke. They never calculated the consequences of their actions, committing sins of omission and sins of commission. They were gamblers, forever trapped by their reptile brain. Insanity."

One name in particular caught my eye. "Is this who I think it is?" I said, pointing to one recognizable name.

Stingo nodded, "Yep."

This was a criminal that had once been on the front page of every newspaper around the world. It was the name of the guy who had shot president Reagan.

Stingo moved his hand contemplatively down the trunk. "These are the names of former brain lab students who refused to grow up." Stingo sat down on his bed. "They are victims of The Cosmic Mafia. Most of them are in prison. Or dead."

I had never heard him use that term before, The Cosmic Mafia. I instantly found it frightening, sinister, and very creepy.

Stingo scooted back onto his pillows which he fluffed and propped up behind his head. He looked content and comfortable and a complete opposite from the picture and point he was making about the people on the tree trunk. I shuddered.

"You can learn how to use your brain and control it, or you can gamble with your fate." Stingo laced his hands behind his head and shut his eyes. "But remember, the universe plays hard ball. The Cosmic Mafia keeps score. You get away with *nothing*."

Chapter 11
Retreat

Time passed and eclipsed into my fifth year coming to visit Stingo at the lab.

I had stayed in touch with him on a regular basis throughout each passing year one way or another. When the spring thaw came like clockwork each season I spent as much time on the mountain as I could. When the way to the lab was often completely blocked by snow drifts in harsh winter I communicated mostly via mail, as for myself, I had neither a jeep nor a mule.

Besides the specific work concerning the brain lab and brain lab projects, I discussed and worked with him on strategies for my own artistic career and creative efforts. Stingo was an invaluable aid given his early rocket-like success in show business. He had a savvy business sense coupled with an inherent psychological understanding of how people's minds worked.

But it was 1986 and the world was continuing its rapid downward spiral towards frightened cultural conformity, increasing economic vertigo, and further moral and physical chaos and oblivion. The Black Monday stock market crash in October had people sweating in their shiny black oxfords and sliding out of their red high heeled shoes. Chernobyl continued to radiate in everyone's minds- not to forget also across a formidable wide swath of the Ukraine. California began its slide into the Pacific with the biggest Los Angeles earthquake in recent memory.

It was all just a matter of time before everything would become unraveled. We were fairly certain of that. But for the folks of the Dormant Brain Research and Development Laboratory, eternally optimistic, all of this bad news seemed like a great opportunity:

Tickled team amygdalae to the rescue! Our grinning gleeful glial ganglion gang would be there to toss out a floating frontal lobes lifesaver to any willing whirling wanderer trapped in the spinning whirlpool of planetary peril.

*   *   *

Over the preceding years I had eventually become Stingo's right hand man. But Stingo knew he had to read me carefully. He didn't want to scare me off, one of his last remaining accomplices.

He knew by now that if anyone told me to do something, I would of course, usually do just the opposite, or sometimes nothing at all. Thus, over the years, he tried to re-educate me through osmosis. He knew that I would absorb information and suggestions more readily via indirect means- What I would pick up as he instructed curiosity seekers who arrived for one or two brain lessons at a class or at a public presentation.

But all did not always go so smoothly.

He would give me an assignment to carry out down in the city, and if I screwed up, he was not shy about letting me know exactly how he felt:

16 Feb 86
Dear Niles:

I was shocked when you told me on 6 Feb that you did not perform the tactical maneuver I gave you in my letter of 2 Jan:

"Make personal contact with the specific person at Westword, Denver Post, Rocky Mountain News, KVOD 6:15 P.M. 'Daily Calendar', KCFR and other such outlets in direct charge of listing future cultural events. Make sure we get listed prior to each of our now regularly-scheduled meetings in February, March, April and May."

156

Overall survival strategy depends upon the trustworthiness of those performing the tactical moves. I am alive today because my trustworthy buddies performed their supporting tactical moves protecting my flanks while I made the strategic drive crawling on my belly through barb wire and mine field at night to knock out the machine gun killing us.

I trust that at our next meeting you will report that you did your duty.

D. A. T. Stingo

I rarely made the same mistake twice.

No, not the same mistake. It was usually a new and completely original one.

He knew I chewed on the information he had me deliver to the local media as press releases, in his infamous "research reports". This was his name for the colorfully descriptive information sheets that he regularly disseminated to the press that kept his name and the business of brain afloat in the public eye.

Stingo could count on me to regularly bring my own friends up to the brain lab. He understood that I carefully watched and absorbed the manner in which he presented his methods and brain-self-control facts to them.

I never did sign on for the full six-week Brain In Nature course that he taught every summer to ever dwindling numbers of students. I just wasn't a "group" sort of guy. But more than anyone over the past few years, I had helped Stingo year 'round, whether it was dragging firewood down the steep mountain side for his winter heat, taking care of publicity down in the city, or helping him to organize and put on public lectures.

I had made The Brain Revolution my own, at least for the present. I had not yet found a reason to drop out.

Not yet.

Stingo kept the heat on me and my brain, to stew the concept of Frontal Lobes Transcendence.

But for most, "Transcendence" was a term that had not well weathered the wilting of Flower Power of the 60's. Further, the decade following Sgt. Pepper that saw the birth of endless bouquets of transcendence techniques proved to be a further disappointing stale potpourri of self-improvement promises unfulfilled.

In the mind of the general public, "Enlightenment" now was a basket of dried out rotten fruit tossed onto the unwanted clearance table, a collection of coconut chotchka statuettes left over from a failed palm tree paradise tourist trap.

Perhaps if Stingo had pared Frontal Lobes Transcendence with "How to Improve Your Stock Portfolio" he might have fared better in the 1980's.

So it was, that despite the dismal state of world affairs, vast hordes of volunteers for The Brain Revolution Army had failed to materialize. It was spotty at best.

Yet, we trudged on, as a team.

As for my solo efforts, I had been teaching more traditional paths of self-reflection coupled with pretzel twisting postures for the previous year at a place called The Yoga and Fitness Center in east Denver. It was run by a diminutive elderly woman named Ina Hamwich. It was the first such far-eastern oasis for meditation and hatha yoga that I can remember. Back in those days Denver was a mid-western city better known calf roping than for standing on one's head. Undoubtedly, it still is.

I had found out about the Yoga Center from a lovely auburn haired flute player I had encountered in my sophomore days in the college concert band at Metro State.

A decade previous, I had changed from a drooling steak coveting carnivore to instant vegetarian trying to get in good with another lovely lass who herself was a plant eating herbivore. Although the promise of a green romance failed to blossom, I stuck to my gums, and never ate another Filet Mignon again. I guess I thought adding yoga to my repertoire would increase my luck with this new little redhead.

Of course, that plan didn't work out either. But nevertheless, I kept up my yoga twisting after the flute tooting puckered out, and made a lot of new friends like Glenda and Ina. When it was time to find a place for Stingo and me to present amygdala tickling lessons to the needy masses, the Yoga Center was a fine facility at our disposal.

We had just finished the third in what was a deteriorating reception for a series of *Brain In The City* presentations. When we had begun the first brain self-control class, the place had been packed with dozens of eager participants who had seemingly bucked the trend of increasing populist materialism. But with each succeeding week's presentation, the group's eagerness for neurological spiritualism had shrunk like a pair of jeans washed in hot water and thrown into the hot drier.

Nevertheless, for this particular cranial dissertation, Stingo and I had optimistically set up row after row of metal folding chairs hopefully for the anticipated audience. Alas, only a half a dozen people had bothered to show up for the final installment.

I gathered up the uncollected brain maps and brain guide sheets sitting left abandoned and sitting on the tops of seats. Stingo, wearing the same out-of-fashion leisure suit that I had seen him wearing on TV nearly a decade earlier, packed up his plastic electrical click switch and plastic brain model and tossed them into a small cardboard shoebox.

I walked up to Stingo and handed him the papers, a distinct forlorn look on my face. He took the papers, smiled, and placed them in an old leather satchel that he clicked shut.

"This is depressing," I remarked.

"Niles, my good man, there's no reason to be depressed. We are learning."

We folded up all of the chairs and stacked them up in a closet off the main room.

I followed him as we walked out the main exercise room and into the front reception area. At the front desk sat a small smiling woman in a black leotard.

"Thank you so much Ina," Stingo said, shaking her hand. "You've been of great help and a gracious host."

In a calm controlled manner Ina replied, . "Any time, Mr. Stingo. It was a pleasure to have you. Namaste."

Stingo opened the front door, delicately accentuated by the tiny jingle of a little brass bell mounted above the door. I followed him out onto the sidewalk.

"Well, let's call it a night and be on our way," Stingo said, taking a deep breath of night air.

"I don't get it," I remarked. "We don't seem to have learned anything."

"Oh, but we have," Stingo countered. "We have learned what *doesn't* work. And *that* is more important than knowing what does." He smiled at me.

The Yoga Center parking lot was adjacent to a yuppie bar. As we stood there, our attention was caught by two men and a woman, all apparently greatly intoxicated, loud and obnoxious. Stingo and I silently watched the woman fall down and lose her shoe while the two un-gentlemen just laughed. They then picked her up by her armpits, hardly managing to stay upright themselves as she, teetering, struggled to get her shoe back into place. A full minute later, oblivious to us, they all barely managed to navigate themselves further down the sidewalk.

"The Brain Revolution is coming, Niles. It must come. Or else the planet will not survive. It cannot survive seven billion dormant human brains."

"It doesn't look good, D.A.."

160

Stingo moistened his lips. "When my buddies and I were in the Battle of the Bulge in World War II with mortar shells flying inches over our heads, it also looked very bad. But in the end we snatched victory from the jaws of defeat. We are also in a war now, Brain Lieutenant Abercrumby. The war to save the planet. And we will win. We must."

I wasn't feeling convinced. "That's pretty idealistic," I replied.

"Of course I'm idealistic!" Stingo reiterated as he pointed at the strangers disappearing down the street. "Without that, what do I have? We would be no better than them!"

Stingo looked at me, and then rubbed his stomach and added, "However, although I may not have a void in my idealism, I have a void in my stomach right now."

Shortly thereafter we found ourselves at The White Spot Café on South Broadway, about a mile from the center of downtown. Tall buildings were visible through the large glass picture window lining the street side. The place was filled with quietly chatting customers, staff, and a few street people who came in from the outside chill to sit and nurse free coffee refills for as long as they could get away with it.

Stingo and I sat at a booth, with him munching on a grilled cheese, myself playing in a bowl of alphabet soup with my Spoon.

"How's your grilled cheese?" I asked.

Stingo pursed his lips together, made a loud exaggerated smacking sound, and made a gesture of perfection with his fingertips. "As fine as the finest French Cuisine as is to be found south of the Stock Yards and North of the South Platte River. How's your vegetable soup?" Stingo politely asked.

I was busy spelling out "E=mc2" as best I could in the broth. "I'm working on it."

We sat there in silence for a few further moments when Stingo gently enquired, "How's your brain self-therapy coming?"

I dropped the Spoon in the bowl, splashing soup and a few errant letters on my face and shirt.

Wiping myself off and picking an N and a Z off of a button, I responded as casually as I could muster, "Good, good."

I probably didn't sound that convincing. I reactively resisted having anything shoved down my throat- whether it was the greatest alphabet soup on the planet or the greatest wisdom in the universe, even if it was from my best friend, mentor, or a combination of the two. This was all about brain *self*-control. I didn't like being told what to do, from my mother, or my brain teacher either. I felt like was a big boy.

But Stingo would push the envelope a little bit on occasion. A public place was a safe bet. He used his sandwich to defuse a potential confrontation between teacher and now *semi*-rebellious student.

"Niles, when you make a habit out of clicking your amygdala forward and you finally pop your frontal lobes, you'll understand completely. People are looking for the answer to life. But they're looking in the wrong places." He started out as casually as he could muster.

"Yeah?" I said, trying to imagine what kind of places he was referring to. "You mean in this bowl of soup?"

Stingo pointed at me with the sandwich gripped tightly in his fist, ignoring me, as if I had said nothing. "The answer is between each set of ears, washed or unwashed."

I looked up from my soup, my eyes first alternating between his ears. I couldn't quite look him straight in the eye. But then he looked straight at mine and grabbed my attention, hypnotically. I couldn't look away any longer.

With total conviction he continued, "You automatically get group telepathy, you automatically get advanced intelligence- You get whole brain POWER." His voice began to resonate to the end of the lunch counter. People began to turn our way to see what the commotion was.

He grabbed my wrist with his other hand. "It's POWER!"

Then, he slapped his own forehead with the butt of his palm, looking a little frustrated and almost angry, "The power in your own head! Take it!"

Now the restaurant had become strangely silent. Everyone was staring at our table. Stingo was completely oblivious. He relaxed and smiled at me, as if a switch had been clicked in his head.

He combed his ruffled hair back with his hand, then continued with nary a pause, "And *once you take it…*" Stingo whistled, as if a bird had whisked off into the sky, "…Higher Reality. This lower reality is a *pain in the butt.*"

Stingo smiled to himself, and took another bite.

*   *   *

I wasn't sure about lower reality, but as far as I was concerned, helping Stingo gather his firewood every fall on a 10,000 foot mountain at a 45 degree angle slope was about as big a pain in the butt as I was willing to tolerate. There I was again that fall, dragging twenty-foot tree trunks tied together with a rope slung around my waist. I was making my way a third of a mile down a narrow mountain trail hauling logs to keep his cabin warm through the cold Rocky Mountain winter.

Trudging down the steep trail with the rope biting into my hips, I reflected on the five years that I now had under my belt with Stingo and the Dormant Brain Lab.

Every month that went by confirmed that my life was fundamentally changing in important ways. The wires inside my own head were connecting in different ways than they had been hooked up for decades previous.

Stingo regularly emphasized the importance of "child-funsie-gamesie". And so I made an effort to re-discover the world from a kid's perspective. I stopped categorizing certain things merely as "little things". To a child, *everything* is important

What we see and what we ignore is largely a result of the psychology of the culture we live in. Adults compartmentalize everything. They categorize certain things as worth noticing and everything else as irrelevant.

I deliberately started paying attention to those things society perceived as unimportant- those things back in the intellectual shadows. I discovered there were whole worlds in there, in the things that everyone else ignored.

I studied the texture of a brick or the way that a doorknob rotated.

And then there were questions that people never spoke of: Why did that man in the supermarket act so funny? Why did some people drive big fancy new cars and other people in old coats sat at the bus stop? Do ants think?

Nothing was off limits within my mind, and unexpected answers came from the most unlikely sources. I came to the conclusion that there were in fact no "secrets" in the universe. Everything under the sun is right there, all of the time, right in front of our noses.

The thing is, everybody has blinders on; people perpetually wear dark glasses that perceptually filter out most of the scenery. These blinders are our cultural expectations, what we expect to see, what we learn to look for.

That's the only *real* secret, that we're all wearing these pitch black goggles, and we think we're seeing all there is to see when we are only seeing a sliver of existence.

The ability that many brain lab subjects and students shared which allowed them to perceive beyond culturally learned boxes and borders was almost certainly due in large part to spending significant time on the mountain. Looking down from outside the city at its goings on from high and far away in the forest gave one an impressive and unique perspective and independence. You just wouldn't see things the same way eating a taco sitting at a plastic dining room table down the street from Big Mac Auditorium.

Historically, there was plenty of precedence for this amplification of awareness preceded by time in the wilderness, in a cave, or in the desert. You never saw the rat race for what it was until you dropped out of it, at least for a couple of weeks. Then you began to see all kinds of things people were in too big a hurry to notice otherwise.

What brain lab people regained was *curiosity*. This is usually lost by the time one gets to high school, certainly upon college graduation, certainly when you've landed your first job, gotten your first mortgage and had a couple of kids. By then you are so pre-occupied with the race for survival and the struggle to hold on to your possessions, that your brain gets scared numb.

I don't think anyone has discovered this yet, but I think curiosity is the result of a chemical that floats around in a child's brain. As kids get older, their brain chemistry changes, and kids lose their curiosity the same way they lose their baby teeth. The chemical is no longer produced and perhaps is nullified by raging sex hormones. Maybe one day somebody will nail the Nobel Prize for naming the curiosity chemical in the brain of pre-schoolers.

As the years went by, I had spent countless hours at the lab listening to Stingo's endless stories, some of them quite wild. I could hear from him first-hand experiences that nobody else could speak about so vividly- like living in the woods for over thirty years, being a national TV celebrity, having fought up at the front lines in World War II, and more.

I had endless questions about subjects that covered a 360 degree dome. Stingo did his best to answer these with his thirty years life senior over me, and he almost always did this in an entertaining way.

Often we sat together way past dark, and I had to slowly wind my way back to the car with real owls hooting. Most of the time I returned home with a satisfied smile on my face and my intellectual curiosity satiated, at least until the next visit.

And every time just as I set back down the trail, Stingo stood at the top of the path twenty feet outside his cabin and did the most unusual thing, something that no one in my life has ever done before- and it was right out of a musical Western movie:

He always sang me a farewell song as I set off, summer or winter, a song his old pal Woody Guthrie wrote long ago. He was as predictable as the seasons in my departure each time. I can still see him on the trail waving good-bye and singing to me...

```
"So long, it's been good to know ya
 So long, it's been good to know ya
 So long, it's been good to know ya
 This snowy old snow is a-gettin' my
home,
 And I've got to be driftin' along.
           SO LONG!"
```

I would always turn back one last time and wave farewell myself. "BYE BYE!!" I'd yell back.

Stingo would laugh. I was as predictable as he was.

Stingo was intensely interesting, a character in my life like no other. I mean, who lives like that? Most people would think, "That's crazy!" He had all that education, had all that TV fame, and still chose to live in the woods without electricity or running water.

He was a pretty tough guy in a lot of ways, not only in how he lived, but in how he related to people on a very direct level. Like I said before, that's how he weeded out the fakers. When people heard about the brain lab's neural adventure they thought, "Oh THAT sounds like FUN. Let's check it out!"

So they wrote to him and maybe eventually made it up to the lab acting like they were really interested in what the place was all about. I saw this again and again over the years: They would say that they wanted to get involved. But when it got down to brass tacks, they were just paper clips- they weren't interested in doing the serious work. They didn't really want to change, they just want to be entertained for a little while like a kid who puts a nickel in the toy horsy at the supermarket to go for a ride. Just playing around, pretending until something else grabbed their attention.

Stingo told me, "Always test for the lie. You can't trust anyone 'till they've transcended into their frontal lobes. The reptile brain will say anything. It will look you straight in the eye, and lie. People will waste your time if you let 'em, maybe half your life, or worse."

He knew how to be social when he wanted to be, when he had to be. But at some point, sooner or later he disposed with the social niceties and demanded that people got serious.

People might briefly think that were fooling the guy, and acted like they wanted to have a real serious discussion. But talk is cheap. Before the fakers knew it, Stingo saw right through the bull, and BAMMO!! He'd cut right to the chase and they'd run like rabbits.

His life was about The Brain Revolution, and if you didn't eventually get around to that, you were wasting the time on his sundial, and he'd bite your head off to let you know. That scared off most everybody.

Stingo always seemed to be testing the water, testing where everyone stood, like a constant experiment. I didn't always understand what he was up to at first, but more times than not, I would eventually figure out his strategy from the sidelines.

Over the past year our relationship had changed dramatically. I had taken on a lot more responsibility for helping out with Stingo's educational efforts. I took care of delivering all of the regional and national press releases. I organized and promoted more public presentations for Stingo and myself. I arranged and did TV and radio interviews.

I benefited by learning what Stingo himself learned becoming a nationally known TV personality. He continued to guide my own burgeoning career as a musician. The guy had been around the block, and he had experience and advice to give that I would not find anywhere else.

It was early September. I had driven up to the mountain to help gather the wood again for the winter heat. I walked up the long familiar steep trail through the now golden forest up to the kitchen cabin. I rang the bell and then continued further up to Stingo's place.

From outside his red door I looked through the window and saw him inside rummaging through one of the file cabinets. When he looked up and saw me I waved hello and I began to let myself in. He stopped me before I had one foot in the door.

"Wait! Wait!" Stingo shouted as he held his hands up in front of my face. "Close your eyes. I want you to close your eyes first."

I closed my eyes tight and felt Stingo hold me by my arm and slowly lead me like a blind person into the center of the cabin. I couldn't imagine what the surprise was.

I heard Stingo step away, and then he told me, "Okay, open 'em up."

I didn't know what to expect, but I figured it would be something unusual at the very least. I opened up my eyes. Stingo had me facing the inside wall of the cabin, the side with the stove and all of the cooking utensils.

I looked carefully. I didn't see anything different at all.

Stingo asked with marked anticipation, "Well, what do you think?"

I just stood there. "Um, let me see…" I kept looking around. I figured that it was some kind of a riddle.

"Well?" he asked again.

"Hold on, I'm still looking…" I scanned the area high above the stove where the extra bunk loft was, then to the side of the stove. I couldn't spot anything of significance at all.

"Gee D.A.," I said apologetically, "Uh… I don't see anything. What am I supposed to see?"

Stingo let out a distinct sign of exasperation. "Look carefully!" He seemed to be genuinely amazed that I was missing something that was so clear for him.

I kept looking, this time crouching down to peer under the stove and into the corner. I looked under one of the tin pots hanging up on the wall, and then I began to lift a pot lid sitting in the middle of his frying pan.

Somewhat exasperated, Stingo gently grabbed my wrist. "No no. It's not under there, sit down." Stingo reached for the step stool that I always used as my chair inside the cabin.

He pointed to the stove, "I spent five hours cleaning that thing. Just for YOU."

"Oh no!" I blurted out.

He shook his head.

Now I got it. I remembered looking at the mess when he had left me up on the mountain all by myself. I tried to make up for lost ground, "Oh! "It looks great!"

Then I realized that although I had previously noticed what a greasy mess the stove had been, I had not actually mentioned it to him. "But, how did you know…" I began to blurt out, but Stingo cut me off in mid-sentence.

"Stop, too late," he said as he waved off my nearsightedness.

The day's real focus was gathering fire wood, not discussing the cleanliness of the appliance that burned the wood. I had brought my portable miniature music cassette player with me that day since I had quickly learned that physical labor up on the mountain was made easier to the sound of music, even if it wasn't Julie Andrews doing the warbling.

As I trudged up and down the mountain that day, instead of torturing my ears listening to Maria Trapp von whatever her name was, I had been listening to strains of Captain Beefheart and His Magic Band. His unique vocalizations had dramatically lightened the load of dragging twenty-foot long fallen pine logs down the long trail.

"Woe is a me bop, Om drop a rebop, Om," sang the Captain to a decidedly angular and chaotic beat heard at full blast through my headphones. Stingo and I passed each other regularly, one of us going up while the other was going down.

Gathering firewood consisting of an almost impossibly exhausting one-third mile walk straight up the mountain in back of his cabin, far past the football field sized rock wall known to us as Eagles' Nest. You could never make it in one go without rest stops every five minutes.

Halfway to the top of Laughing Coyote Mountain you would start to look around for already fallen dead and dried out trees. There was a seemingly inexhaustible supply of them up here among all of the healthy standing pines. I never once saw Stingo cut down a healthy tree, and these were plentiful. He did occasionally bring his chainsaw up to cut off the side branches, because you had to do this in order to successfully drag each log down by sheer foot power.

You did this task by tying a looped rope around one, two, or three logs bundled at one end, and then wrapping the other end of the thick rope loop around your waist. Then you started tugging. It was the hardest work I had ever done in my life, and it remains to this day the hardest work I have ever done. Not only was it completely physically taxing, but the mental obstacle to keep going when every muscle in your body protested "Enough!" was as big a block as anything to overcome as well.

If there were any branches still sticking out from the truck, they would immediately get hung up on any of the thousands of small rocks buried immovably and randomly down the trail. So, Stingo did his best to cut these all protuberances off. However, something would always be left on sticking out a little bit. You would get some momentum going for thirty feet, almost at a run, and all of a sudden it was like an elephant putting on the brakes.

"ARRRGGGGGGG@!!!!!" I could periodically be heard to proclaim among the twittering birds.

It was completely unpredictable. And getting stuck completely tested your ability to overcome the inevitable frustration of having your downhill flow jar to a sudden halt at any moment by a teeny little bit of branch not cut perfectly flat to the trunk.

I think there are many things in life exactly analogous to that.

Reminiscing about Stingo's little piece of the wild, this reminds me of the pine beetle infestation that has been increasingly killing off thousands of acres of trees throughout the Rocky Mountains.

For decades, the forest service has been scheming largely unsuccessful ways to manage what has now come to be recognized as a disaster of epic proportions where upon millions of acres of pine trees will eventually fall victim to these deadly little worms. There is nothing anyone has yet figured out to stop it, perhaps with one exception.

I had noticed from the very first that Stingo's neck of the woods was a perfect picture-book example of what I would imagine the mountain woods to be. Here there were no wide stands of brown pine trees at all, commonly seen in the mountains. It tuned out that this was exactly one of the reasons he had claimed that the brain lab was exempt from personal property taxes for so long.

"This is a farm. It's agricultural property and I'm growing trees. Further, I'm running a long term scientific agricultural experiment involving a basic natural resource," he told me, matter of factly.

"Everywhere in the mountains you see pine beetle kill, except at the brain lab. We don't have that problem here because I'm managing it with *consciousness*. The national park service forest should be taking classes from me, they should learn brain self-control. You can stop pine beetle kill with pure consciousness."

That fall afternoon as we were harvesting the brain lab's woody natural resource, I finally ran into Stingo at the side of the trail sitting in the shade of one such uninfected tree. He waved me to sit down, "Relax, take your time."

I happily sat down.

"Only work to 60% of your capacity," he advised. "More than that, you burn up your coils, it's inefficient."

We sat for a while and enjoyed the relative warmth and the light breeze.

"Just look at 'em all, down there…" Stingo pointed east, far away in the direction of the high plains, where the metropolis of Denver sat as far as the eye could see. "Running around in the maze, and not a handful can explain to you a what for."

He took a long deep breath. "This is the only life worth living, in the bounty of Mother Nature," he said. "And the only job worth having is being an artist."

Stingo considered himself to be a writer, first and foremost. That day, however, no writing was being done. It was a day of non-intellectual brute physical force.

We sat for a long time, and didn't say much. Eventually I voluntarily pushed myself up. I knew the drill, I knew the routine, and started my way back up the mountain to fetch some new logs.

I turned around and asked, "Where is everybody anyway. How come I'm practically the only one who helps you with this any more? "Where'd all the old brain staff and graduates go?" I had looked through the records and archives, and had seen for myself photos of Brain In Nature alumni from the 1970's and earlier. I had also peered at case studies in some detail from the file cabinets in the archives.

"Aw," he said. "Once they pop their frontals, Fffft! They disappear, and I don't hear from them again."

I knew this wasn't completely true, as the mail he got was still quite substantial, even in the mid and late '80s. I still heard familiar names from time to time. But here in 1986, the souls who were now physically venturing up to the mountain were few and far between, save what few friends I brought with me from time to time.

He looked at me a smiled, "You're quite the exception, Brain General Niles. You don't know how much I appreciate it. Thanks." He gave me an impromptu salute.

Although I had apparently earned a promotion in the ranks, I laughed at the absurdity of the idea; myself as a officer of any brain battalion. As hard as we tried, I think in the end we were both staunch individualists to the core.

We trekked up and down all day, and by four o'clock I was completely worn out. We stopped for some hot black tea back at his main cabin, and after a short while I took off and drove the long familiar winding route back home along Clear Creek.

I arrived at my front door, went inside my apartment, and began to empty out my back pack. Suddenly, I realized I had left my valued new walkman cassette player up on the trail.

I rummaged through every corner of my pack, but sure enough it was missing. I then remembered exactly the place on the trail I had taken it off and set it down in some grass. "ARG!" I exclaimed to myself.

Such a thing was quite expensive back in those days, and this was a super deluxe version that I was crazy about. I knew that if I didn't go back up there that minute it would be ruined within a day or so from the weather, or it would be lost to a kleptomaniac ground squirrel mistaking it for a big nut.

Reluctantly, I hopped back in my car and drove the long drive all the way back up to the brain lab. I barely arrived with just enough light left to keep me from tripping over every rock on the trail going back up. Even so, I had been smart enough to bring my own flashlight just in case it took me a while to find my player.

I was confident that I could relocate the spot where I remembered putting my player down, and indeed after a long strenuous walk back up without even stopping to greet Stingo first, I found it, exactly where I had remembered leaving it.

I had never begun a visit at night before, and by then it was already quite dark. Nevertheless, on the way back down the trail, at the last moment I decided to knock on Stingo's cabin door.

His cabin was pitch black inside. There wasn't even a kerosene flame flickering. But from inside I could faintly hear the radio playing classical symphonic music in the void.

Although I couldn't make him out, I was fairly certain Stingo was lying in bed, and as was his habit he had tuned into KVOD. This station was known as the "Classical Voice Of Denver", the only station he confessed to listen to. It was still broadcast from the very same small brick building where Stingo had started his own career first as a radio announcer before hitting it big on TV, almost forty years previous.

I tapped on the door, knock knock knock.

The music continued.

"D.A.? Hello?" I asked, not too loudly.

The music played on without a stir.

I knocked once more.

Knock knock.

Nothing.

"Hello, Stingo. It's meee..."

I waited a good minute or so and listened for any stirring.

I figured that the guy must have been out cold, completely exhausted from all the tree dragging we had done earlier.

Finally, after hearing no movement at all, I shrugged my shoulders, turned around, and started off towards the trail leading down to my car. I thought it a little odd that he wouldn't hear me and get up.

But before I turned the corner on the trail, I suddenly heard the door about thirty feet behind me creak open in the dead dark silence. In the faint moonlight I could vaguely see Stingo standing inside the cabin's doorway.

He said nothing.

I figured that in the dark he had no idea who I was. After all, how could he begin to think that I had driven and then hiked all the way back up to the mountain so many hours after leaving.

"It's just me!" I said, knowing that I would have surprised him.

There was a long silent pause, so I moved towards him standing in the door. I could begin to make out more details. I stopped about twenty feet away.

I shone my light in his direction for a moment. To my utter amazement, I realized that he was wearing a coonskin cap, one of his red flannel shirts, but no pants at all. It was strangely comical, almost.

However, it proved very unfunny within a few seconds because of the fact that he held something quite large, long, and darkly ominous in his right hand. I couldn't tell exactly what it was, but it looked like either a long axe, or worse, a rifle. I couldn't exactly tell which. He wasn't smiling.

I instinctively lowered the beam.

Then he said something completely out of character. Upon hearing it, the hairs all stood up on the back of my neck.

"Retreat." He said formidably.

"What?" I stammered.

He said it again, louder and more forcibly this time, "RETREAT."

I suddenly realized that perhaps he didn't yet realize it was me. "It's me, Niles," I offered. "I forgot my cassette player up on the trail and I came back to get it." I shone my flashlight on my face, and then on my player.

Another short pause was followed by one word, unmistakable, and without any question of its intent.

"RETREAT!" Stingo slowly raised the object slightly in his hand.

Now I was shaking in my sneakers. I stared for a moment at the thing he was beginning to hold up, squinting to make out what it was. Here it was, nearly pitch black, miles and miles from any other human being, and Stingo had completely lost his mind. Either that, or I didn't know this guy half as well as I had thought I had all of these years.

All I could think was, "I am going to *die* any second..."

As calmly as I could muster in the face of an apparent complete lunatic, I said the only thing that made any sense to me...

"Okay then, I guess I'll get going... haha... see you later."

I wasn't going to argue with him, and I wasn't going to stick around to ask him what that thing in his hand was.

I turned on a dime and made off down the trail as quickly as I could without breaking into a literal sprint. I knew that the worst thing you could do was to run away from a mountain lion who was eyeing you as his next meal. From the sound and look of Stingo, I had no idea whether he planned on mounting my head above his stove or not. But I surely wasn't curious enough to find out.

I had never gone back down the trail to my car as fast as I did on that night, and I continually looked back over my shoulder to see if I was being pursued to my potential skinning.

I was in complete shock. None of this made any sense at all.

It was with stupendous relief fifteen minutes later that I found myself locked safely inside my station wagon, and that I had not left my lights on and drained my battery.

The car started up and I backed up out of the rough parking area out to the dirt road, praying I wouldn't hit anything sharp with my tires. "Please, oh please..." I muttered to myself.

I rushed back to the main highway as fast as I dared. I drove home, all the time wondering if I would ever return.

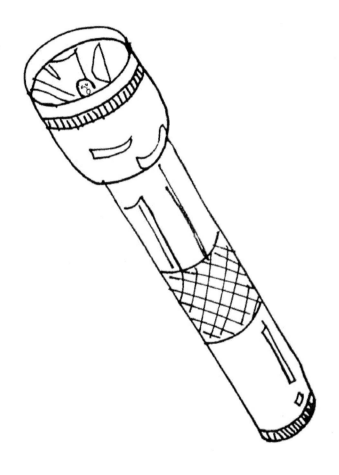

Chapter 12
Silence Is A Cookie

Stingo's bizarre and completely unexpected behavior had shaken me enough that I let the rest of the year go by without returning to the lab or even writing to him.

Was this The Cosmic Mafia beginning to rear its ugly head, channeled through D.A.T. Stingo? Were there things about him that I had never suspected, that he had secrets hidden from me that might prove unexpectedly fatal at too fast a moment's notice?

I had no idea. At the very least, "Retreat!" was a clear sign that I should at least spend a few months contemplating things completely on my own.

For the past year I had increasingly felt that who I was, who I was meant to be, and the fulfillment of my life was not dependent on Stingo or anyone else for that matter. I would stand on my own two feet. I would survive regardless of what would be tossed at me, and that would include incomprehensible behavior by my brain guru who for the moment signaled to me on no uncertain terms to make myself vanish.

It may have been that I needed time alone to think for myself, time to really test my independence without even Stingo peering over my shoulder.

It could have been anything. Was this the You-niverse testing my self-reliance to the core? Or was Stingo deliberately and unexpectedly ambushing me and testing my coolness in the face of utter fear for my life?

Was it a big brain lesson I didn't yet understand?

Frankly, I couldn't answer any of these questions and unexpectedly I was no longer sure about where I stood with Stingo.

Three months went by without a major hitch, and also without hearing a word from Stingo. The faith in myself had not been shaken completely loose.

By the end of the year I finally got an itch to go back to the lab to see what was what. I couldn't envision that dreadful dark encounter would be the end of things between us. It was a mystery that would have to be resolved one way or another.

So one morning, I made up my mind to venture back. It just happened to be the day before Christmas.

Just for insurance, I stopped and bought a couple of cold night warmers for Stingo as presents- a bottle of 101 proof Wild Goose Chase Bourbon and a bottle of the Stolen-Itchneeyah Russian Vodka. I wasn't going to show up empty handed.

In Colorado, clear roads in the mountains can be found to last far into the winter, and the eastern foothills are known for days of reaching 60 degrees or more in January. It wasn't quite that balmy on that day, but I had little trouble navigating most of Smith Hill Road even though it was already well past the winter equinox. Finally, near the top, I did have to walk the last mile up a snow covered portion of road; it was just too much for my little twenty year old Japanese car.

I trudged another half mile from the road itself up the lab's final dirt trail, which now was nothing more than a narrow path of snow. Arriving at the kitchen cabin as I had countless times before, I rang the bell. This time however, I didn't know what to expect, but I was ready for anything. I was prepared to run like a deer on steroids. I certainly wouldn't walk further up without a clear signal to proceed.

I stood there for several minutes, and then suddenly heard the familiar call to come up, "Woot woot woot!" Stingo signaled in his recognizable owl impersonation.

I methodically continued my way up to Stingo's place. Upon arriving I could see some smoke snaking out of the tin wood-stove chimney pipe that jutted out from the side of his cabin. From an angle of about ten feet away I looked through the window. To no surprise I found him back inside on his bed, just removing a page from his typewriter and then crumpling it up.

As I had seen him last time standing at his door scaring the wits out of me, he was wearing the same old red flannel shirt. However, to my great relief this time, he was also wearing pants. It was winter, after all.

I took a deep breath, walked up, and not knowing what to expect next, I resolutely knocked on the door. He immediately looked up, recognizing me.

There was a pause, and my heart stopped for a moment. Then he smiled a big wide grin, "Hello Niles!" and he greeted me with great enthusiasm from beyond the threshold. "Come on in, come on in!"

I cautiously thought to myself, "Okay, so far so good." I opened the door and stepped inside.

"Just cleaning out the old house," he said pointing to his head. He then stood up from the bed, opened up the stove door and tossed the paper ball inside. "What brings you here this wintry day?" he asked with a smile.

"Well, it's been a while, and I figured it was about time to come back up here," I said, weighing my words and giving no hint at how freaked out I was last time I saw him. "Happy Christmas, or New Year, or whatever," I said, holding out the two big bottles in front of me.

"Okay, okay," he said. "Thank you, thank you." Stingo took the bottles, and simply put them up on a shelf and said nothing more about them. I knew he liked Vodka, especially when it was as cold as a Siberian ice cube up on the mountain. I also knew that he would never let anybody drive back down with even a drop of alcohol in their blood.

"Great to see you," he said with a note of real sincerity. "I thought you might be coming up sometime soon." He glanced up at a dog-eared calendar hanging on the wall, then silently pointed and counted to himself as if calculating a formula. "Yep, today seems about right. Come on outside, I've got something to show you."

He slipped on his boots, and I followed him out the door. I began to breathe normally and my apprehension began to melt.

I hadn't planned this trip at all. I hadn't written to him. I hadn't even considered coming back before that very morning. The fact that Stingo said that he once again had a premonition that I would show up completely unannounced was doubly unexpected because my trips to the lab well into the winter were generally rare.

Stingo's behavior months earlier had been a complete and disturbing riddle that I had turned over in my mind countless times. I assumed that eventually I would confront him with finding out what his bizarre behavior was all about, and on no uncertain terms I would do it only in broad daylight.

But now, here I was, and Stingo was behaving as nothing at all had happened.

He acted so genuinely happy to see me, he acted so absolutely cordial that I didn't want to even breach the topic. I didn't want to disturb the calm relief that I felt that everything appeared to be completely normal between him and myself.

We got outside the cabin and Stingo led me around to the side where he had kept a small covered metal trash can under the eaves of the roof. This was his backwoods refrigerator.

"Here, look here," he said as he removed one of the lids. "I've put plenty of fresh snacks and food inside this."

I looked inside, and there were boxes of crackers and cookies, a Jar of peanut butter, and other treats.

"Any time you come up here and you're hungry, just help yourself to anything you find whether I'm here or not."

"Oh wow. Thanks a lot, that's really nice." I replied. He opened a carton of cookies and offered them to me.

I was used to bringing up my own lunch and such, and of course I had partaken in a rare organized meal. But this was different; this was a specific gesture of intimate friendship towards me that had nothing to do with the formal work at the lab.

"Have one now if you want. Have as many as you like."

I gladly took a couple of cookies. "Thanks a lot," and I didn't hesitate at all to start munching away. They were chilled but not frozen.

We started a casual conversation as if nothing had ever happened. I had never seen Stingo so casual and so overtly friendly towards me, or towards anyone else for that matter. This was nothing short of remarkable. I had as good as forgotten about my forced retreat on that dark night months previous.

I am the sort of guy who is nearly incapable of backing down from a challenge. And I will say that I have wasted countless hours of my life wrestling with people over absolutely inconsequential trivia.

I have further wasted countless hours of my life engaging in winning battles that meant absolutely nothing in the end.

And although that night three months earlier my safety might have been in serious jeopardy- or not- the truly intelligent thing to do at that moment confronted by a coon skin capped mountain man telling me to "Retreat!!" seemed to simply make like a mouse and scamper away to live another day.

Madman or not, Stingo had a cabin full of sharp pointy objects, and well, I only had a plastic tape player in my coat pocket at that moment.

Perhaps the event was not a trivial matter at all, that it actually *was* monumentally important beyond my comprehension. But it also might have been nothing more than a hiccup, a single slipped tooth gear in the rational mind of a guy who was the most rational person I had ever known in my life.

Maybe he just had too much vodka that evening before bed.

Heck, maybe he was simply sleep walking back on the battle field of the Arden. Maybe it was a once every fifteen year post-traumatic nightmare in the middle of the night up on a mountain where there should have been nothing more than insomniac rodents looking for abandoned marshmallows. That explanation seemed more reasonable than anything.

I will never know, because I never did bring it up, ever, perfectly content to leave it forever alone. Let smiling sleeping dogs nap.

I had passed a crucial test.

Chapter 13
I Popped My Frontals

September 11 1987
Old Oak Writing Desk
Printer's Cabin
 The Dormant Brain Research and Development Laboratory
Blackhawk, Colo, USA, Earth, The Milky Way

To whom and whatever brains it may concern,

Yesterday I popped my frontals down in the city. I came
up here as quickly as I could to tell Stingo about it.

It (popping my lobes) took a bit longer than I thought it
would. It's been maybe six years sincxxe the first day I came
up to the lab and learned about my reptile brain with a bucket
over my head.

But Stingo was smart--- He knew how to make you remember
something important without making it too painful.   ;-) He
was a tough teacher. But sometimes you've got to be cruel to be
kind. (But I would say Stingo was never "cruel" just "tough").

Touydxxx (typing mistake arg..)

today he was up on the trail getting firewood, and I hiked
up to him. We both sat on a big flat rock in the middle of the
trail and talked for a while.

I remember that HEHsxxxxxxx he told me long ago, 'When
somebody pops their frontals, I burn their flies xxxx arg --
FILES " "I burn their files". I don't know if he meant that
literally, but I think he meant it metaphorically- that he
didnt have to worry about that person any more. You've grown
up.

So I symbolically gave him a book of matches.

I don't need his or anyone else's approval any more.

Whew.   This is my graduation, and I gave myself my own diploma by giving him the matches. Light away Stingooooooo!

He smiled, and asked me a couple of questions, like "Is your ego still as big as the Cherry Creek Reservoir?"   I kinda laughed, but I told him "No!" anyway just to be on the safe side.   He congratulated me and then suggested that I go down to the printing cabin and write down a few things while it's all still fresh in my mind.   So here I am using one of his old typewriters to hammer out my immediate thoughts. (but wish I could type bettter.)

It would be like if you tried to explain to somebody the taste of strawberries. You can quite never quite do it until theyve got a mouthful of berries inside their OWN mouth- but what the heck, I'm going to try:

Yesterday, it was THE BIG LIGHT BULB going off. They call this "Popping your Frontals" at the lab. I'll never forget it. S so THIS is what he's been talking about. THIS is what all the other people were talking about in the movie I saw a long time ago

It was SO OBVIOUS.

What was it like when a huge surge of current blasted forward from my puny reptile brain past my amygdala into my prefrontal cortex?

Imagine your sitting at the bottom of a leaky wooden row boat looking for a shortcut to China lost in the middle of an endless ocean for what seems eternity, back when they didn't even know the Earth was shaped like a golf ball.   You're just waiting to fall off the edge of world into oblivion. Then all of a sudden, out of nowhere......

YOU SEE LAND! HOLY COW!!!!!!!#2@!!

Only this wasn't a chapter in some history book.I didn't
expect it at all. I was just doing some work at my friends
recording studio, fixing some wire connections-....
   WOW-thats SO APPROPRIATE...
Anyway, I was doing this work not even thinking about my brain
and all of a sudden it was like being shot out of a cannon. I'm
sitting there on the floor hooking up these wires behind the
control panel, and suddenly
                    I GOT IT.
   Duh.
In three seconds I mighrtxxxx
   In three seconds I might as well have been accelerating
through the galaxy in the nosecone of a rocket ship. And yet
 there I was, just sitting on the carpet with the pliers in my
hand. All my previous worries were no more important than
whether I would have whole wheat or white breadtoast for
breakfast. Too funny, really.
   It's so weird because if anybody else had been in the
room with me they would never know what was going on inside my
head except for maybe this huge grin on my face,this look of
c omplete astonishment.
      It took me a long time. I am SO DENSE. Ha it doesn't
matter now. I always expected popping my frontals to be
something else out of my reach. But only I-me-myself could know
what it was, for me.
      Maybe if I had been around more of the other brain lab
gfxxXx students, but I'm kind of a loner, and most everybody
else from the old days are gone. Maybe in the end that's
actually better. I"m more independent and I didn't do this to
fit it with the crowd. I wasn't hopping on any brain band
wagon. I didn't do this to impress anybody or to fit in with a
group.

      I've been coming to this brain lab -lets see--- First came
up in early summer 82, its going past five into my sixth year
now or however you figure that. Didn't follow the instructions

for the longest time I really didn't do what Stingo told me I
was supposed to do(all the brain game exercises) until just
recently.

I Didn't even try the memory reprogramming (Self-trauma
drama)brain exercise till about a month ago when I sentxxx went
out a few times driving down I-25 yelling my brains out and
getting all the old forgotten bad feelings out of my brain. A
couple people driving past me must have thought I was crazy. (I
figured I better not do that exercise in my apartment or
somebody   would call the police from all the yelling..)
I mostly just hung around, watched Stingo and listened to him
barely getting my toes wet. I saw a few people come up here in
the summer and do the brain camp, but not too many at all.

Da stingo startedthe lab in '57, and hundreds of people
had come through, and he had tested all his theories and
hypothosises. Hypothesis hypotheseses. But by the time I
arrived, the research was done. Stingo had been working mostly
on his own for the past few years at that point and he was
spending the majority of his time just writing and sending out
a few papers and press releases, doing interviews here and
there, trying to educate people. Most people in the city who
had even heard about him thought he was just   a crazy old
hermit up in the woods. A few people got it, but the big Brain
Revolution he's talked about hasn't come. Not yet anyway. Guess
that's the human race for you. Most haven't crossed the neural
finish line. Most don't even know it exists.

As for me- I knew somehow that there was something to all
of this all along. Maybe it was just trusting this mad man to
be not so mad after all in the end.

I've spent the last few years helping him so he let me
stick around even though I didn't exactly follow the directions
or 'read the instructions' like he told me the first time. He's
been my friend, and so I tried to be his.

He's done his best to tell people about what is inside in
every brain waiting to be discovered- but heck, you can lead a

horse to water, but people? Forget it. But I guess now we'll still keep trying, together.

I plan on doing a lot more now myself, I'll keep bringing up friends so they can maybe see what this is about. I'll try to learn more myself. I practice my typing too.

But really, I don't know exactly what I'll do, or where this will all lead-

You-niverse, SURPRISE ME.

Chapter 14
The Dusty Trail

Two more years flew by. It was 1989 and Stingo and I continued to try and jump start The Brain Revolution in whatever way we could. But yet, things progressed ever so slowly.

I had landed some big solo concert gigs, including one at the Gerald Ford Amphitheater in Vail where I attempted to show two-thousand Republican golf tourists how to tickle their collective amygdalae as part of my show. I called it "A Night of Mind Music". But nobody was jumping on the Brain Bandwagon yet.

Stingo and his ideas, namely brain self-control, were perceived as a mere curiosity. He remained an eccentric in the eyes of the press, who utilized him when there wasn't an interesting enough murder or war going on and they needed some column inches to fill.

Eventually, something became crystal clear to me: There was a disconnect between what my own experience with Stingo at the brain lab was and what people were getting through Stingo's own words and writing.

I cannot overemphasize the positive impact that all of my time together with Stingo had upon my life. There was a thread that existed between myself and my brain teacher- no, this is wrong. It wasn't a thread, it was a six-lane highway.

Something passed between Stingo and me when I was up on the mountain that I found irresistible. It was like being addicted to bolt lighting. Even the times when he was up on the mountain and I was far below in my little apartment in the city, every letter that I opened up in great anticipation was a prize that contained a jolt of inspiration and change.

It was easy to understand the powerful energies that existed in the incredible natural environment in the wilderness, but I had always assumed that Stingo had translated this powerful life-altering electricity in his writings, his books, and in his personal letters via his WORDS.

Nope.

I finally realized that this wasn't the case.

The reasons why this became clear to me was that I was the principal messenger of Stingo's press releases delivered to the mass media. Few people were getting from Stingo's own writing what I was getting from Stingo himself

It finally dawned on me that Stingo's own writing style was so idiosyncratic that his manuals and reports remained practically incomprehensible to everyone else- certainly to the man on the street.

What I was getting from Stingo and what I had learned from Stingo had little to do with what he was putting on paper- but had everything to do with what lay beyond the page.

He could have written me nursery rhymes, stuck them in an envelope, mailed it to me, and this probably would have had the same effect.

The fact was, I was tuned into the guy's high band ultra-violet frequency, and I was seeing beyond the words to perceive the deeper meaning of his lessons- precisely because of my actual time together with him.

I got his quirky sense of humor and use of language. But more often than not, it might take me MONTHS to make any sense of what he was tapping out with his old Smith-Corona.

For anyone else, his manner of writing was just so bizarre, unconventional and weird, it was more of a turn off than an inspiration to just about anyone else. He could be verbose and vulgar, and his humor could easily come across as adolescent and/or old fashioned and corny.

One afternoon years earlier I had received a city assignment from him in a letter that subtly, yet clearly demonstrated his troubles getting anyone to seriously consider what he was all about.

27 April 84

Dear Niles,

Can you please do me a little favor and go to the library to compile a short list of about 20 paperback book publishers? You can get them from the book, WRITER'S MARKET. I need the names of paperback publishers who would be interested in printing a manuscript, "Neural Economics." Their description in MARKET would have to seem to indicate they are interested in receiving business and economics manuscripts.

I have exhausted all the hard-back publishers, receiving rejects from all. So get me the names of exclusively paperback publishers. Print them out neatly with name, address and one line of their description which indicates why they might be interested in this neural approach to changing the capitalist system from brain-destroying drudgery to frontal lobes transcendence for all workers and mangers on the job--- to transforming America.

Love
D.A. Stingo

And in the years following, nothing really changed. In fact, things seemed to get worse. Nobody was getting the REAL MESSAGE of brain power from the very guy who was Mr. Brain.

Here was the Pied Piper of Brain Self-Control, and nobody was listening to his tune- at least not in the numbers that Stingo was so desperate to reach, i.e. everybody else on the planet. It was a disturbing and frustrating thing for me to see. Stingo's own writing was sadly ineffective for the masses.

The conundrum I faced finally resolved itself on a slow satisfying walk back to my car from Stingo's cabin one summer night in 1989. The biggest treat I got was not something Stingo had safely tucked away in a pail outside his cabin- it was something I found tucked away inside my own head, something that began to add up in an equation that would ultimately only reveal itself fully later on.

What I finally realized was that Stingo's Typewriter was tool, a CONDUIT for transmitting energy.

He was conducting something through his Typewriter- something that totally changed the landscape of my experience, something that transported me to another You-niverse entirely.

This energy took shape in the sentences that he wrote-

But it wasn't just in the *literal content of his sentences.*

It was beyond that.

Stingo was a great friend. He was the most amazing teacher. But unless one managed to have some kind of personal experience with the man, you could read his research reports all day long and scour his book manuscripts-and you would just end up scratching your head. One had to look beyond the page. Otherwise, at worst, you might think all this talk about brain self-control was a bunch of hooey.

Stingo's You-niverse was not the same place every one else lived in. His Typewriter was both a gateway and a guarded portal to another reality.

Few were willing to brave the gauntlet to pass; few were willing to leave the comfortable lexicon of the familiar to explore what lay beyond.

And so, as brain work became an increasingly more prominent part of my own creative efforts, my own frustration also grew. I couldn't continue to just bang my head against wall after wall trying to get others interested in what I was experiencing. Something had to change-

I decided to write my own brain book. I would pare down my experiences and what I learned at the brain lab and put it all in a short volume that any person could pick up and read in a couple of hours. I wanted to create a simplified text, in more or less plain English for all age readers.

I would summarize the methodology created, evolved, and used by Stingo at the brain lab since its creation nearly four decades earlier. My hope was that anyone would come away with the basic information, a direction to proceed, and an idea of where it was all leading to.

And I would do it in a way that would offend no one.

I would not let words trip over their own feet.

I would make it all fun.

One morning as I began an eight hour drive home from visiting a friend five hundred miles away, I stopped at a flea market outside of Durango to buy a soda. As I walked around looking at all the old things, I spotted a tiny hand held cassette tape recorder. I instinctively bought for a dollar. I just can't resist gadgets.

As I held it in my hand, I realized that this would be the perfect opportunity to summarize everything that I had learned from Stingo and at the brain lab, and to put it down, so to speak. I bought some extra batteries and found a few extra cassettes.

For eight hours, from behind the wheel as I drove through the mountains back to Denver, I dictated into the tape recorder everything that I could recall about brain function, the triune brain, and clicking my amygdala forward. It was as simple as that.

The following week upon my return I typed out a transcription, and Voila!- I had my very own first brain book.

I adapted all of the lessons I had learned to my own simple language. I presented it all in a light and non-aggressive manner that I was used to in communicating with beginning music students. I expressed rudimentary ideas and stories that I felt everybody could easily relate to. After all, I already had thousands of hours teaching music and art behind me by this point, and I had been making my living on average suburban and city streets for over fifteen years. I knew what people could digest and what they would tolerate.

Upon my next visit to the lab I showed it to Stingo, and he was absolutely delighted. We sat together on several occasions and he helped me to tune up my writing in a way that I agreed was even more effective.

I got to practice my typing.

It is somewhat ironic that Stingo's own writing never met great acceptance, but that my own book would years later eventually land me on international radio and television shows, and would achieve the notoriety that had proven so elusive for the man who originally coined the term, "Clicking your amygdala forward".

Stingo wasn't much of a musician, but he bought a mountain playing three chords on a guitar.

I wasn't much of scientist, but I would make a career out of publishing books on pop neurology.

Life is funny that way.

A couple of more years went by. My own career was making some nice progress, and I was starting to build a local reputation- perhaps I should say infamy- for my unusual music and my equally unusual musical presentations, like my Upside-Down Saxophone Concerto or the Einstein Taxicab Quartet. But those are mostly stories that I will save for another volume.

In the fall of 1992 I took one of my oldest and best friends to visit Stingo and the lab. This was Frederick "Vincent" Poindexterity who for years went by the name Eric Vincent. This came from the name of one of his favorite painters, Vincent Van Gogh.

We made a trip up to the lab in the fall to do some firewood collection, as well as to meet with Stingo and to share with him our new and continuing plans of rock and roll immortality. You see, Fred and I forever had dreams of fame and fortune in the musical universe, besides anything else we would do. Eventually we made a CD together, and on it, Fred ended up writing and playing a song called "The Click Song". It was all about clicking your amygdala forward, and he played it on D.A. Stingo's very own 1959 Vega Banjo.

After Fred and I had finished dragging down what must have been half a ton of firewood, we sat around inside relaxing and shooting the breeze with Stingo and talking about the future. Somewhere in the conversation, Stingo referred to our musical efforts as "brain revolutionaries spreading brain know-how". At that Eureka moment Fred exclaimed, "That would be a GREAT name for a band!" And so, *The Brain Revolutionaries* were conceived, later to be realized with a couple of my music students. Eventually it generated a pop album titled *Amygdala Brainbites*. It was ear candy for the brain.

But it was also in his cabin on that fateful day moments later that Stingo voiced his clear intentions to eventually will the brain lab and all its contents to me when he died.

"Some day this will all be yours," Stingo stated matter of factly to me. "There's no one else. You'll need to be ready, and you'll need the help of people like Fred and your students to teach the world how to evolve into their frontal lobes."

Not only was I overwhelmed to hear of Stingo's intentions to make me the legal heir to all of his property and the brain lab, but was astonished that one day I would have the deed to such a huge parcel of wilderness. It was incredulous and totally unexpected.

By that time I had spent over ten years aiding Stingo in every way I could. For all intents and purposes I had become his primary assistant to spread The Brain Revolution. On my own, I had incorporated brain into my own music, my performances, my efforts towards publicity, and into the very core of my life.

I considered Stingo's Brain Revolution as my very own, and he expressed it as such that fall afternoon

When I got back to Denver, I excitedly told everyone what Stingo had said to me, that he was planning to pass the mountain on to me one day. The following afternoon I called a good friend, Raquel Baegel, and invited her to a game of miniature golf to share the news with her.

Raquel was the single mother of two girls whom she had hired me to teach piano lessons to. The older of the two would eventually become a singer in *The Brain Revolutionaries* years hence.

Raquel leaned over her putter, lining up a long drive down the green felt putting fairway. "Niles, Get it in *writing*," she commanded in no uncertain terms. She hit the ball, but instead of following it, she looked at *me* with a scolding mother's eye.

I dismissed the notion as I put my own golf ball on the rubber tee-off mat. "What? Come on, I don't have to do that, I don't have to worry. Stingo's doing fine. He's not going to die any time soon. He told me he planned to live to a hundred and fifty."

I felt like she was worrying about nothing.

"Oh, now I see. Now you want to be a gambler," she scolded.

I felt like she was lecturing me.

"Niles, listen to me. GET IT IN WRITING."

I thought she was crazy. I thought she was being paranoid. I didn't even give it another moment's thought until I talked to her a couple of weeks later over the phone.

"So Niles, did you listen to me? Did you get Stingo to put it in his will, *in writing*?" She gave me the third degree from the other end of the line.

"Of course not," I laughed. "There's plenty of time for that. He's not even 70 yet. He's got another eighty years at least. Stop worrying."

It was ridiculous.

However, the new year had Stingo facing problems he had never anticipated in his worst mountain man nightmare. Something new had reared its ugly head in Gilpin County, and it was a serpent that even his advanced frontal lobes were not able to wrestle down: Overwhelming Community Greed.

Just as I had glanced in the Blackhawk newspaper headline in the guest cabin only a few years earlier, Colorado citizens had since overwhelmingly approved of turning the tourist trap of Central City and neighboring Blackhawk into a trap of another sort: Casino Fly Paper.

In recent years, mountain top community slot machines and blackjack had become a reality, and it was growing at a rate faster than the pine beetle population explosion. People desperate for good luck were streaming into the casinos like horse flies, leaving the contents of their wallets stuck inside the glittering walls of gambling halls, twenty-four hours a day, three-hundred sixty-five days a year.

Central City had become Pinocchio's Emerald City with sparkling slot machines and green carpeted card tables. City Hall was drinking from the bottomless tax-base well of corporations that were making millions upon millions from gambling's permanent new headquarters among the pines. It was a new gold rush that would have had the original Gilpin County gold panners blush in embarrassment from their comparatively modest fortune hunting.

The idea of something for nothing and the timeless fantasy of sudden yet totally improbable wealth had replaced the simple rational understanding that the statistics and odds were overwhelmingly on the side of the rich Casino owners.

Nothing would get in the way of gambling profits. Certainly not a crazy old man in the forest who publicly labeled legalized gambling as nothing more than an explosion of reptilian greed in his relentless press releases about The Lack Of Intelligence in the Colorado Rockies.

What this all meant for Stingo and his brain lab was utter disaster. The local government had promptly increased his property taxes 2000 percent to force him off the land that he had called home for over thirty-five years. The casinos and their friends in land development had artificially raised the land value of all homes in all of Gilpin County and they were looking for new residents who had deep pockets rather than residents with deep character. Stingo would have to go one way or another.

He fought on as best he could, but by early 1993, he had run out of options. He had fought to keep his property taxes as they had been for the previous three and a half decades. He had taken his lonely battle all the way to the Colorado Supreme Court- and lost.

There was really nothing I could do. I was as broke as he was.

Nevertheless, I trudged on promoting The Brain Revolution on my own terms and in my own individual way, even if it meant Lingo might lose the mountain and that I would have to put him up on my couch.

I hoped to get a foothold in the public consciousness through music and entertainment, the very elements and tools that Stingo himself had used to acquire the very mountain, the property on which the Dormant Brain Lab had been built and begun.

Stingo had been enthusiastically behind my efforts for the musical version of The Brain Revolution ever since I had morphed his ideas with my own. In January of '93, he had written at the end of a ten page correspondence-


```
Now, once this scientific defense perimeter is
secured, then your secondary musical troops, "The
Brain Revolutionaries" can be absolutely guaranteed
of $ucces$$ via your creatively correct strategy and
tactics: "Less words! More pictures! More MUSIC!
Brain/Frontal-Lobes/Amygdala! Click! FUN!!"
```


A couple of months later, having been absent in person from the lab most of the winter, I followed up again with a brief note to Stingo telling him of my latest music project's progress as I was wrapping up my very first CD album…

Dear Stingo,

Hope you are enjoying the warmer weather. Album production is in its very final stage. All of the parts have been recorded and I am mixing down to stereo, the final product, getting the balance of parts in perfect equilibrium. It will be "candy for the ears and food for the brain." Not a bad slogan. I expect this step to take another week and then its all done…

…Hope your end of The BRAIN R/EVOLUTION is going well.

P.S. People love the name, The Brain Revolutionaries.

Later, love
Niles

Several weeks went by and I anticipated getting a response any day.

One afternoon in the middle of the month I received an unexpected phone call. It was a response, but not exactly the one I had expected.

"Niles, this is Hannah Kardbord. How are you doing?"

"Okay. And you are?"

"I was a friend of Stingo."

This instantly registered as ominous. She had said "was".

She told me a little bit about herself since I had never heard that name before. She went on to tell me that she was a former brain lab student from the 1970's, and that she had been coming back and helping Stingo in his tax fight over the past year or so.

This was news to me. I had known that Stingo had attempted to represent himself in court, but I didn't know of any other people helping him in the matter. I also knew that Stingo kept certain things to himself, even from me, so I took her at her word.

"They found Stingo's body in one of the cabins a couple of weeks ago. We're having a ceremony next week and I wanted to let you know about it."

She explained that Stingo had apparently suffered a heart attack, and had fallen and struck his head on the corner of the printing press machine in the printing cabin. She said that he was found by a couple of teenagers roaming around on the property.

I was in shock.

Suddenly I remembered his unexpected defense posture and his command to "Retreat!!" the night I had startled him out of his sleep.

"How often had people disturbed him or threatened him?" I asked myself. Is that what that night was all about?

He had never complained of heart trouble.

How vulnerable was this old guy living completely alone up on a lonely mountain?

The following Saturday I trudged up to the lab and found a half dozen people there that I had never met before, including one of Stingo's nephews who was now laying legal claim to all of the property and all of the goods.

Only a short time earlier, Raquel had warned me.

I had gotten nothing in writing.

*   *   *

I didn't know what to make of things, and it was a blow to have seen the lab and all the property slip from my hands completely and irrevocably, given Stingo's clear intentions only months earlier.

We were told that Stingo had died of a burst artery. We were told that he had a heart defect that had gone undetected. At least that's the explanation we were given by the Gilpin County coroner.

He had died in the same cabin where he kept his printing press.

I think it broke his heart, perhaps quite literally, that the masses were ignoring what he had spent his life formulating, and then printing in his years of monthly research reports that too few were reading, and even fewer taking seriously.

Although he had claimed to have answered the riddle of why he had to kill his brother in the war and presented a cure for that disease- there were still too many amygdala clicked backward towards too many reptile brains. There were still plenty of wars to go around.

People wanted to take what remained of what little he had

It was too much.

At the mountain ceremony Stingo's nephew was there representing his own father, Stingo's brother. The extended family lived in California, and Stingo had only ever mentioned any members of his family in only the slightest passing remark. He had little contact with his blood relatives over the years, but now the state was awarding custody of everything to the brother. Regardless of his intentions, there was nothing legally binding to indicate that Stingo wanted it any other way.

There was absolutely nothing I could do, and the state law was clear about stipulating that the legal heir was the nearest next of kin unless arrangements were clear and in print.

Eventually I would be awarded Stingo's Martin guitar by the family after proving his clear intentions for me to have this object to aid in *The Brain Revolutionaries* brain music thrust. I would also be given permanent custody of the infamous brain in the Jar, originally the property of Stingo's neurology professor at the University of Chicago. And by that, I mean the professor's personal neural property- it was in fact the brain housed inside his professor's own cranium, left to Stingo when the professor was done using it.

One former staff member was leading a team of a few other former staff to lay claim to Stingo's papers and intellectual property and they were negotiating with the estate to retain rights to Stingo's writings.

I had not met any of these people before, and I politely refused invitations to join a newly formed coalition of former students and staff. I had not seen nor heard of any of them during eleven years previous, save one person, and even that was only on one or two brief occasions. I was not enthusiastic about forming a new coalition with complete strangers no matter what the cause.

I would independently continue the work I had done for the past eleven years with Stingo, alone.

One new person I met at the scattering of the ashes was a pleasant young woman that I soon recognized as one of the original brain lab students prominently featured in the Stingo documentary film. Her name was Harmony Anise, and she had been named by Stingo as Vice-President of the Adventure Trails Survival School. That executive decision was made in writing fifteen years earlier. She ascended to the seat of President of the brain lab corporation by legal default even though any last contact she had with Stingo was a score of years earlier and years before my own arrival on the scene.

Adventure Trails was the legal name of the brain lab corporation, even though it had for all practical purposes been referred to as the Dormant Brain Lab since the late 1960's. Stingo had long ago set up the lab as a non-profit tax exempt educational institution, and on paper it remained Adventure Trails. Even so, I wasn't aware of any other people involved at a corporate or legal level as administrators or officers. There certainly weren't any board meetings.

None the less, despite an absence of any such meetings for at least a dozen years, Harmony quickly began to organize an effort to insure the safe keeping of Stingo's legacy, and we saw eye to eye on most everything in this regard.

Together, we quickly retrieved as many critical papers and documents off of the property as we could. A couple of vintage musical instruments and that infamous brain in a Jar had already been collected for safe keeping. Unfortunately, by the time anyone had arrived on the scene, looters had already made off with all of Stingo's war memorabilia as well as some chainsaws and a few firearms that he kept on the property, and those were never seen again.

No will was ever found, except one lone uncompleted mail-order Do-It-Yourself Last Will and Testament Kit that was stuck in the back of a file cabinet. Apparently Stingo had never really gotten around to taking it seriously. The last time I talked to him about his life-span, he figured that brain self-control still gave him another eighty-five years on the planet before anyone would be fighting over his wrinkled remains.

He certainly had not planned on leaving anything to any surviving family members with whom he had minimal contact, long deserted lab staff, or anyone else that I knew of. This was made pretty clear by the scribbled note he left on the front cover of the will kit. In the typical way that he enjoyed thumbing his nose at everyone, especially people who unfairly believed were entitled to something, he wrote this, in big bold letters...

I am taking it with me.

Chapter 15
Another Jar

A week after flinging Stingo's ashes into the mountain breezes, I had a spectacularly real dream. It was one of those remarkably clear and lucid dreams that make you sit up in bed completely astonished. I had Traveled via my frontal lobes into a parallel dimension.

I was back up at the lab, and in the Library cabin with Stingo standing behind me. He had his hands on my shoulders and turned me to face out a window, through which he pointed.

"Go there," he implied with only his gesture, indicating out into the forest, not saying a word.

Suddenly from the distance behind me, I heard a bell ringing, the school bell on top of the kitchen cabin. It rang and rang, continuously. I immediately noted that it didn't make any sense at all to me, because that bell went "Ding! Dong!" This sounded more like a buzzer.

Suddenly, I bolted up in bed.

It wasn't the kitchen cabin bell at all. It was my doorbell.

Still in my pajamas, I went and peered out through the little peephole in my front door. There stood the tallest cop I had ever seen, maybe about six foot five. I grasped my pajama strings.

I had no choice, and so opened the front door, but only about nine inches. "Yes?" I stammered, talking through the screen door.

"Are you Niles Abercrumby?" the policeman said with a blank expression and foreboding tone.

"Uh, yes sir. What's the matter?" I quickly made a survey of all of the potentially illegal activities I might have engaged in over the preceding weeks.

"Did you write this book?" The cop quickly held up a copy of The Frontal Lobes Handbook for me to see on the other side of the screen door, a copy of my very own brain book that I had begun selling at the local book stores.

"Uh... uh huh..." I squeaked.

"Well," he continued, "I saw this at the library."

"Okay..." My face twitched.

"And I bought my own copy. I was wondering if you would autograph it for me." He smiled.

I grinned a nervous smile of some relief.

"Sounds strange, but some of us policemen do think about other things besides crime."

"Oh yeah," I responded, "of course, sure you do. Haha."

This was just about the last thing I expected. But I invited him inside, quite nervously eying the closet in my living room.

"Can I use your bathroom for a sec?" he first asked.

"Oh sure, right here!" I pointed, right off the front door, urging him to go inside as rapidly as possible.

I ran into the living room and quickly shut off a humidifier and florescent lights that were on inside of a closet there. I quietly shut the door.

I had recently been reading about Gordon Wasson and his travels to the remote regions of the Yucatan Peninsula in Mexico. Wasson was the first European, or white person, or whatever you want to call a non-native American, to attend an ancient curandero mushroom ceremony. This was a supernatural healing practice that had been performed for hundreds of years in the high Mixeteco Mountains of Mexico. The secretive ceremonies remained completely unknown to westerners until the nineteen-fifties.

Visiting my local botanic gardens, I had stumbled upon an exceedingly rare copy of *Russia, Mushrooms, and History* by Valentina Pavlovna Wasson and her J.P. Morgan bank vice-president turned anthropologist husband Gordon. Shortly after I had been given permission to pour over this printed volume in a locked up cage of a room at the garden's library, I began studying the ancient mushroom eating cults of southern Mexico for myself- in the mushroom flesh as it were.

Like the Wasson couple, I too was interested in Travel of all sorts. But unlike that banking CEO, I was too broke to go much further south than Colorado Springs. So I did the next best thing and followed in their footsteps, albeit in the comfort of my own living room closet, where for a short period of time I was cultivating the magical fungi for myself.

Stingo had never let anyone do that sort of thing at the brain lab, but this was my own apartment, and my own brain lab.

I felt a bit of nervous relief and then heard the sound of running water from the bathroom. The cop emerged pulling his pants up by the belt. "Coffee and donuts… you know… heh heh."

I scribbled my name in his book and he gave me the thumbs up sign as he left. I locked the door behind him.

Despite the close call from farming forbidden fruit in my closet, the dream I had been interrupted from implicitly indicated that there was still something at the lab waiting for me. Although I didn't have a clue what that thing might be, I would drive up the next day and find out exactly what it was.

Everyone had abandoned the lab for the time being, and I found it much in the state that it had always been save the obvious rummaging through that one would expect relatives to do upon looking through a long lost uncle's belongings looking for hidden gold.

None of Stingo's relatives were ever interested in his work or even his private life beyond a cursory curiosity, and they all considered him just an eccentric old hermit up on some Colorado mountain best left to his own devices. So, most everything was untouched. The papers and uncountable odds and ends remained where they had been left by Stingo.

Of course, I remembered the treasure under his bed. But that was already gone. By the time I had even been notified of Stingo's departure from this sphere, one of the former staff members had already absconded with it. I was later fed the tall tale that the silver dollars were used to pay for his cremation. Although I knew this was a load of mountain goat manure since Stingo's family had borne all funeral costs, I would freely admit that disposing of a rotting dead corpse would qualify as an emergency use of Stingo's stashed funds had this actually been the case. It hadn't been.

I made my way to the scene of my dream on the mountain. This was the Library archive cabin which sat about fifty yards behind and uphill from Stingo's main residence.

Inside, the Library was an intriguing place, more practically recognized as the tool shed. It had been where Glenda and I had been shown Stingo's war souvenirs so long previous. Even more confusing, however, was a sign that hung outside the door that said "SKOOL". The sign of course, was written in Cyrillic, even though I had never known any instructions being given there in any language, save instructions for oiling a chainsaw.

Most importantly the cabin contained boxes filled to the brim with thirty years worth of magazines, press clippings, as well as file cabinets filled with detailed records of student and subject studies and experiments. Further, the cabin was a three-dimensional physical scrapbook filled with memorabilia from Stingo's life, including record albums, the original 16mm film documentary that I had seen on TV, and a couple of old broken guitars in need of repair.

But rather than sifting through things, I was more interested in investigating the content of my inter-dimensional night time journey. I walked over to the single window facing the side of the hill on the east side and looked out.

Everything looked normal. I didn't feel any extraordinary sensations or sounds.

"Hmmm," I thought. "Maybe it was nothing, just a dream."

I walked outside the cabin and stood below the window, first looking back inside through the unwashed panes of glass, and then turning around and looking across the wood.

What had Stingo been trying to tell me? I couldn't completely believe that the dream meant nothing at all.

I began slowly walking in the direction that I had faced from inside. Although I had been coming to the lab for years, there were still many unexplored areas on the nearly three hundred acres of wood that were totally unfamiliar. In the forest, you don't have to go more than thirty feet to encounter a totally new perspective.

I walked maybe about twenty yards away from everything. There was nothing out in that direction at all but thick trees and deep shadows. I had never come to that part of the lab before because it didn't seem important. I was nearly at the base of the monumental Eagle's Nest Cliff, seeing nothing except a lot of vegetation. The route to the top of the cliff was far up the hill.

Suddenly, a glint of bright light caught my eye from about seventy five feet away. At first I thought it was a bright electric light, but I knew that didn't make any sense at all unless Stingo had buried some electric lines I didn't know about. But that was a completely improbable. Other than a small broken windmill generator outside the printing press cabin that hadn't even been hooked up for a dozen years, there was no electricity up there at all.

I walked toward the light very curiously, squinting my eyes to make out what it was. I dipped my head one way then the other to get a different angle and then I realized it was a reflection of sunlight off of something shiny upon a large tree trunk.

The tree was a large pine tree at least a hundred feet tall. I walked up to it and first saw that dangling off of a lower branch was a long iron linked chain that had served as a play swing. I impulsively held a few of the links and swung it a little bit.

I realized that the light had been merely reflecting off of a long thin metal strip nailed onto the tree trunk. It had lettering embossed upon it. It was one of those aluminum strips that Lingo had stuck around the lab for students to ponder.

Stingo left these little aluminum strip sayings on tree trunks and odd pieces of equipment here or there so you would run across them unexpectedly. You would have to figure out what they might meant. Many were short riddles, or perhaps unanswerable koans that would inspire one to contemplate something at any time or place.

Aluminum stays fairly bright for a long time and this strip could have been made decades ago. Considering it had always been sitting outside twelve months a year in extreme mountain weather, it still only had a little bit of weathering on it, protected all that time under the boughs of the tree.

The lettering was hard to read, and it was placed about three feet from the ground. "Maybe this was for the kids to read," I said to myself, remembering Stingo's kiddie sized cabin door.

Then I carefully inspected the label and ran my fingers across its surface, almost like trying to make out the words as if they were in brail writing.

The aluminum was about the thickness of a can of soda, and nailed to the bark by two old rusty nails on each side. The letters were raised only slightly from the surface. I could just make it out if I tilted my head to catch the optimum amount of angled light. In all capital letters it said:

I stood up and shook my head. I couldn't believe what I was seeing.

"Control or Chance", I repeated to myself.

The timing of this last lesson from Stingo from beyond the grave was perfectly timed.

The lesson was clobbering me over the head every bit as hard as if the tree itself had fallen over and whacked me on my noggin.

I had the entire brain lab in my back pocket, all 250 acres, free and clear.

But only if I had gotten it in writing.

Instead, I had gambled.

I had left it to chance that I would have years to take care of insuring that Stingo could happily fulfill his good will and intended word.

This was something of such spectacular promise and importance: Ownership of the entire Dormant Brain Lab. I should have made sure this priceless future was safely controlled.

But I had left it to chance.

I sighed the biggest sigh this side of the Continental Divide. I was sure that I would remember those three simple words nailed to that big tree for the rest of my life.

"Ah well," I sighed again, "No use crying over a spilled will." There had to be a reason for it. One day I would figure it out.

I started looking around a bit more. Most of the labels were placed through the lab property in relatively conspicuous places, but this one was strangely in a spot where you wouldn't think anyone would come across it unless they were lost.

I looked further down the trunk of the pine and noticed that there were a couple of bricks covered by leaves and moss sitting at the base of the tree, just between two roots. I thought, "How odd, what are bricks doing here?"

I tugged at one of the bricks, digging my fingers in as much as I could. Although the brick was lodged in place quite firmly, it did budge a little bit. My curiosity was getting the best of me, and so I pulled at it little harder.

Then I heard that scraping sound that bricks make when they slide against each other. It was coming loose.

I sat down crossed legged and really started working at it with both hands. Within fifteen seconds I had pulled the entire brick out, moss and all. I looked down the hole, and to my amazement there was something else there.

It didn't take too long once the first brick was out. Soon I had pulled out a couple more that seemed to form the top of a small chamber.

I put my head closer, sneezed a bunch of forest floor debris up my nose, then peered down. I could make out that inside the small cavern sat the top of a Jar, maybe about six inches down, nestled tightly between the tree roots.

I stuck my hand down the hole and began to tug at it. In one quick "Shooooop!" the Jar pulled free from the roots and the bit of dirt holding it in place.

"Wow!" I exclaimed. I had found a little buried treasure. I was mildly flabbergasted with my discovery.

I stood up and held the Jar in both hands, turning it around slowly and looking inside. It was a pint glass mayonnaise Jar with a severely rusted lid. Obviously it had been buried for quite some time. Inside there was a scrap of paper.

As I turned the Jar in my hand I could hear a tiny little clinking sound and saw that it also contained a little key. I could detect absolutely no mayonnaise, dried or otherwise.

Written on the outside of the Jar all around the circumference were a half-dozen hand written "8"s, but printed sideways in the way that mathematicians write the symbol for infinity. These were written in permanent bold magic marker ink, something that could be seen in nearly every corner of the cabins and upon Stingo's notes, index cards, and signs.

The lid was on quite firmly, as it was a bit rusted. I couldn't simply unscrew it. I first rapped the lid on a rock nearby, although carefully as not to break the glass. Then I bent over holding the Jar firm between my knees, and finally got the top loose. I took out the note and walked into a sunnier spot a few yards away to read it.

"Oh no," I said. The note had one word printed on it, and it was in those same darned cryptic letters that Stingo had used to keep the meaning hidden from most lab visitors:

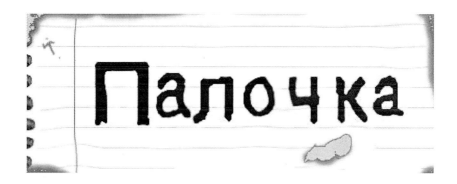

On the back of the paper it had another scribble, but in plain pencil, and in plain English. It said

Hidden In Sight – Looked At But Missed

I certainly couldn't read the Cyrillic word, but for some reason, the pencil scribbling on the back side sounded vaguely familiar, although I couldn't put my finger on it.

I flipped the paper over and over, and I stared at both sides for a good two minutes trying for the life of me to figure out what on earth either meant.

"Okay, this is not unsolvable," I realized, at least in regards to the Cyrillic letters. I knew Stingo's cabin had a ton of books, and somewhere in there must have been a Russian to English dictionary.

I took out the key. It was a small key rather than a house key.

I looked at it, but within a few seconds I clumsily dropped it on the ground.

"Oh crap!" I said. The ground here was covered with thick plants and leaves and I had to dig around for half a minute before I felt it with my fingers.

"Whew." Relieved, I carefully stuck it deep inside my pants pocket.

I went back to the tree and knelt down next to the hole. I looked one more time to make sure there wasn't anything else down there, and there wasn't. I took the bricks and neatly put them all back and then covered them all up with a little bit of dirt and pine needles. I wanted to leave this little spot the way I found it more or less, in respect for whoever left the treasure.

But I darn sure wasn't going to leave the Jar, the note, or the key.

I headed back down towards the main part of the lab, and within five minutes I was inside Stingo's of cabin scrounging around for a Russian to English dictionary. It didn't take very long to find, it was on the shelf right above the Typewriter next to the bed.

There were actually several dictionaries there, including an English to Spanish one, a French dictionary, and even a Portuguese one, although I never heard of any Brazilians or Portuguese coming up to the lab. I guess Stingo was prepared for anything.

The bed springs creaked loudly as I sat down on the bed, the note sitting next to me. I had never looked up any Russian words before in my entire life, and it took a little while going back and forth from the book's table of contents and the index with all the Cyrillic letters to identify what I was actually looking at.

After about ten minutes of struggling, a bit frustrated by wrong alphabetic turns here and there, I finally figured it out.

The dictionary translated the written word as such:

WAND

"Wand? What the heck? What's he talking about?"

I scratched my head. This didn't make any sense at all. I had never heard Stingo talking about any kind of Wands or anything, nor had I seen him waving any such thing around.

"Oh wait… wait," I thought. I remembered the Baton that Stingo had left in his box of war souvenirs. I wonder if that was what he was referring to. "Ah, but that's all gone," I realized, remembering I had been informed that all of the war stuff had been stolen off the mountain already.

I put the dictionary away, went outside the cabin and began to wonder what all of this meant. Immediately I thought of the treasure box under Stingo's bed, hidden inside the stones.

I went back inside the cabin and knelt down next to the bed and pulled the drawer out.

It was still there, but of course the box was now emptied of its silver dollars. I checked to see if the key fit the box. Nope, that wasn't it. I pushed everything back in place.

"What else could this key fit?" I pondered.

There were three file cabinets in the cabin. I tried every one, and it wasn't the key for those. I then thought of the guitar case, but I already had that at home, and it didn't have a lock on it anyway.

I crawled up above the bed into the bunk loft to see if there was anything laying around or hidden up there. Nothing.

I looked around to see if there were any boxes or cases in the cabin that I could have missed, and I didn't find anything.

"Where else, where else?" I looked around the cabin, and I could not think of any place that I had not looked. I started to go over in my mind any of the places on the property that would have keyholes. Nothing to do but to start hiking and find out.

I went to printing cabin first, because Stingo had begun staying there at nights for the last year of his life. Maybe if there was something important I would find it inside.

I went through every square inch of the place. I couldn't find a lock to match the key nor any reference to the note whatsoever. I did find a dead mouse and a few interesting odds and ends including a little box that I took with me. It said "Mousers" on it, although at first I hadn't a clue what that meant.

"Oh, maybe that's where he put caught dead mice until morning!" I speculated, Stingo tossing out the little corpse into the weeds for a bigger hungry critter's breakfast the next day after getting up.

I then walked clear over to the bathhouse. Nope, nothing there.

"Where else, where else? The jeep! The jeep glove box!" I headed over to the jeep, still parked up hill from the bath house and across from the garden.

I slid into the passenger seat and stared at the glove compartment lock, somehow feeling that this would be it.

Tried it.

Shucks.

"Okay, where else? The kitchen cabin?" That didn't seem a very likely place to put something secret and special. I jogged over to the kitchen, and soon was looking in every corner nevertheless. The kitchen wasn't very big inside and within a minute I knew I wouldn't find anything.

I was totally baffled and ready to give up. Maybe it was a safe deposit box key. I had absolutely no idea what bank, if any, that he might have such a box. It would take some asking around to find that out.

I was pretty disappointed that my treasure has so quickly deflated into a wild goose chase.

I walked outside the kitchen and leaned against the outside of it, my head tilted and my and hand resting against one of the logs that made up walls. I glanced at all the graffiti left by lab participants over the years. After so long, I really didn't notice it much any more.

And then I saw something I hadn't paid any attention to since my first day at the lab.

On a segment of the wall sheltered from direct weather by the slanting roof, was a little drawing of a sheep herder holding a long staff. Next to him stood a funny little caricature of a sheep. Underneath the cartoon was an arrow pointing away to the west side of the lab property. The drawing was pretty faded now. More than ten years had passed since I had looked at it long ago on my very first visit to the lab. But I could still read the caption underneath:

"H.I.S. L.AB.M." >>>>

For a few moments, as I had originally thought upon seeing it eleven years previous, I thought someone just didn't know how to spell "lamb".

I stared at it for about ten seconds and then it hit me…

"*Hidden In Sight!! Looked At But Missed!!!* That's it!"

I stepped away from the wall and looked off in the direction that the arrows pointed.

"Of course! The guest cabin!"

The guest cabin was the most isolated structure on the lab. The guest cabin was far away from everything else, nearly on the fringe of the property. Certainly, if there was something to hide away from the prying eyes of visitors or lab students, that would be the place to put it.

I started off across the property. Within minutes the existence of the rest of the brain lab quickly vanished from view and from my mind.

Chapter 16
The Mason-ish Temple

The aspen trees on this part of the lab were thick as could be. The trail to the guest cabin was like a thin thread winding through and missing a stack of needles. But the trail was used so infrequently that it completely disappeared before I arrived at my destination. For the last few hundred yards, I even doubted if I was going the right way.

Then at once I could begin to see the red roof poking up from behind the stands of aspen trunks. In a few minutes I arrived at the porch steps. I looked up at the small red framed attic windows right below the center of the roof, and they looked just like a couple of little eyes with square glasses on. I walked up the wooden porch with a quick rustic clunk clunk from the weight of my anxious feet, walked up to the door, opened it accompanied by a squeak of the hinges, and went inside.

Everything here was neat as a pin, exactly as I had remembered it from my last visit to the spot. That had been when Stingo had left me all alone on the mountain that one day so many years previous. Of course, the dust was a fair amount thicker over everything because hardly anyone even knew about this building, and even fewer ever came here- if anyone at all. It was as secretive as anything was at the lab. Certainly, no one dusted the place. It more properly should have been called "The Guestless Cabin".

I looked around to see if there might be a box or something that the key would fit, but that possibility was settled within a few seconds. There was practically nothing in this cabin at all except an old newspaper (the very same one I had looked at last time) the bed, a chair, and a small table with an oil lamp next to the window. I sat down on the bed.

I sighed, again somewhat disappointed. I was resigning myself to the fact that I would have to ask a member of the old staff, or maybe even Stingo's relatives if anyone knew about a safe deposit box and that I had the key. Naturally, if that was the case, whatever would be in the box would be revealed to everyone, and I wasn't so thrilled with that idea.

I glanced up the ladder that led to the attic. There was the closed hatch. I squinted at it, and there I saw the little brass padlock that I had seen and had left alone years before. I had forgotten all about it.

I reached into my pocket as it dawned on me that this might be the key to open it.

I stood up and quickly went over to the ladder. I immediately saw something that I had not noticed on my last visit. Barely visible was another drawing of a sheep on the side of the ladder. This sheep had an impish little smile on his face.

I quickly scurried up the ladder and tried the key in the small padlock. This had to be it.

"Hey!!!" I exclaimed loudly as the key opened the lock. What you are looking for is always in the last place you look.

I unfastened the locked, removed the key, and put it in my pocket carefully. Then I slowly pushed up the attic door.

The dust was incredible, it got into my eyes and I sneezed immediately- And I am a world champion sneezer. Once I get going, nothing will stop my nasal explosions until I put *something* up to my nose like a tissue or my sleeve. Otherwise, I just keep sneezing and sneezing. And that moment was no exception.

I had to close the attic door above my head and pull the shirt out of my pants and hold it to my nose since I didn't have anything else. I nearly fell off the ladder in my attempt, but I grabbed the side rail and kept myself from falling onto the floor.

Once I stopped sneezing I started up again, this time first closing my eyes and holding my mouth tight. As I pushed up the attic hatch a few dead moths and flies came down. I thought it had to have been twenty-five years since anyone had gone up there.

As I cracked the port open and poked my head up into the dark, at first all I could see were the two small square attic windows from the inside this time, and two little patches of bright sky filtering through them.

It smelled like solid dust. The light was diffused through the cloud I had just raised. Additionally there was something in front of each window on the inside that diffused the light. I could barely make out the shadow of objects up there, but I decided that I would certainly need some more light.

After just a few seconds of squinting in the dark I went back down the ladder to see if I could find something better to light my way.

Back on the first floor I looked around, and quickly grabbed the glass wick lantern on the little table. There was an old box of wooden kitchen matches there too, thankfully. But as I picked up the lantern I realized that it had no fuel in it, not a great surprise at all.

"Well, Stingo's got some kerosene up at his place," I said quietly to myself, as if someone was by my side. "Let's go!"

I laughed at the absurdity of talking to myself, but now I was more curious than ever about the contents in the attic, having found the note and the key.

I knew full well how Stingo loved to make up games for brain lab participants, although I didn't expect to find anything particularly valuable in the attic. But this hunt was especially gratifying given that it looked like no one at all had ever even figured out this riddle and made it that far. The dust alone was witness to that.

I anxiously headed back uphill in order to fetch some lamp fuel. I would continue this hunt to its natural conclusion, and do it properly lit. Before long I arrived back at Stingo's main cabin.

I went inside, poked around and quickly found exactly what I was looking for: A can of kerosene fuel. Actually, it was a gallon can of Wesson cooking oil with a masking tape label that said "Lamp Oil" written in Stingo's special curly cue fancy writing, but in English. I didn't want to lug the whole thing all the way back to the guest cabin, so I looked around for an empty Jar to fill. In a moment found that as well next to the stove.

I filled the empty Jar with lantern fuel, screwed the lid back on, and took off again back down the trail. In a while I was back at the guest cabin.

I had been at the lab enough that I knew not to try and refill a lantern inside because you could spill fuel on the floor, and maybe your shoes, and then before you knew it, you would be roasting yourself like a burnt campfire marshmallow. This could, practically speaking, spread to all of the furniture, ultimately the cabin, and even perhaps a good portion of the National Forest. So I grabbed the lantern and took it outside, and sitting down on the ground I filled the lantern there. I looked around and easily found a covered metal pail with rags in nearby, as most cabins had, and I wiped off the outside of the lantern dry. Then I went inside to light it.

The wick sputtered a few times and then lit steady with a yellow arc of a flame. It put off those familiar outdoorsy kerosene lantern fumes with just a hint of smoke. I adjusted the little wick-wheel until a nice bright light emanated from the lantern, and I replaced the stained glass top. I grinned with delight at my minor accomplishment.

"Problem intelligently solved," I thought to myself.

I slowly ascended the ladder again carefully holding the glass lantern in one hand and steadying myself up each rung with the other. Nervously I imagined dropping the lantern and setting the whole place ablaze anyway.

Then I realized, "Man, I should have gotten a flashlight instead!" I realized I wasn't such a genius after all. Oh well, I was this far, and I wasn't going back for a flashlight now.

At the top, I balanced carefully and pushed up the attic hatch until it plunked open with another rousing, yet slightly diminished chorus of dust and moth corpses.

I held the lantern up ahead of my head and then poked my head up and started to look around. What I saw was completely incongruous to every other scene I had ever found at the brain lab.

It seemed as if I had discovered Aladdin's Cave filled with jewels. All around me glistened reflections and refracted light in every direction. The colors were predominantly blue, aqua, and green, but other colors like orange, purple, and others were also plentiful. I tried hard to make out exactly what I was looking at, and I couldn't quite do it yet.

The problem was that it was very bright outside, and I had hurried so fast to come inside and up into the attic that my eyes hadn't adjusted fully, so I couldn't yet make out any of the details. I had to wait for my eyes to slowly adjust to the light.

I carefully set the lantern down on the attic floor and pulled myself up into the space, and then stood up.

BANG!

"Ow!!" I yelled. I had hit my head on the center rafter of the roof. There wasn't enough room up here to actually fully stand up, and I had to bend down a bit. "Dumb idiot," I confessed.

I kneeled down on the floor and tried to decide whether or not to shut the hatch because I didn't want to accidentally back up over the hole and then fall through it to break my neck. Up here, I might lie around for weeks only destined to become squirrel meat. I decided it was better to close the hatch.

After I shut it, I looked up to see what all of these jewels were, the source of all of the reflections. I began to make out some shapes. Carefully, bent over and crouching, I walked over to the little attic windows.

I had the distinct impression that I was crawling around the interior of someone's skull, and the two windows were the eyes seen from the inside.

In retrospect, I don't think this was very far off the mark.

What I gradually realized was only slightly less astonishing than finding a treasure trove of precious jewels. Instead, what I found was the most amazing collection of glass I had ever seen.

"Whoa," I stammered privately. I could hardly believe my eyes. This was far better than I had expected to find. There were shelves all around the attic, just like the book shelves in Stingo's cabin, and they covered nearly every inch of attic wall space. Each shelf was crammed full of glass Jars and Bottles of every size and shape.

Moreover, I was particularly amazed to find among them a type of uncommon glass object that I had collected as a kid, antique telephone Insulators. This was an unbelievable coincidence.

However first, there were Jars and Jars of all types, but especially Mason and Ball type Jars.

"Heh heh," I laughed to myself. "It's a Mason-ic Temple".

These were the kind of Jars your grandmother might can jelly in. These were mostly all clear glass or blue tinted glass, some with embossed brand labels, some plain. Some of them were tiny, others were typical pint or quart size. However, I found a few of them were unbelievably HUGE. I had never seen anything like the big ones before, and I could not fathom what on earth they were intended to keep. Watermelons?

They all had lids screwed on them or hinged and sealed glass tops, but not a single one had anything inside. Some additionally had extra dried out masking tape wrapped around the top as well.

The other glass objects I knew I would get around to examining in a second. But the Jars caught my attention first because they out numbered everything else.

I picked up one of the peanut butter sized Jars and held it up to my face and turned it around. There was a date scribbled on it with the ubiquitous magic marker, and it read "1.14.60". There was nothing at all inside.

I began to unscrew it, but stopped myself short. I imagined for a second that it contained some sort of experimental gas, perhaps a bug killing formula for specimen collection and that a few weeks later the local newspaper headline would read, "Second Person Found Dead In Abandoned Mountain Cabin From Unknown Gas In Big Jar".

I shrugged my shoulders. "What the heck", I decided without much more contemplation. With some effort the Jar came open, I carefully poked my nose to the edge of the open Jar and took a very quick small whiff.

No smell whatsoever. Nothing.

I stuck my whole nose down the Jar and took a good healthy inhalation. It was indeed completely empty. I sealed up the Jar and looked around, and picked up a few more Jars. Nothing. Every single Jar was sealed, and empty. This was entirely puzzling.

Suddenly however, I felt dizzy in a way, but not dizzy in the normal sense. For a moment it flashed through my mind that there actually had been some sort of noxious substance inside, and that I had just not given it enough time to act. I sat down on the attic floorboards and closed my eyes.

What I felt was a recognizable sensation of movement in every direction. I felt like my body had coalesced into a perfectly round sphere, and I was expanding outward in all directions at once. I had felt this way many times especially as a child when falling asleep in bed at night. This happened just before drifting off to sleep, and similarly upon awakening in bed in the morning not quite fully awake.

It was not an unpleasant sensation, but rather strangely euphoric. In one sense I wanted to hold onto something, but knew that if I tried, the movement would stop.

The speed at which I felt I moved was indescribable. I could have been journeying to the edge of the solar system for the sensation that completely engulfed me.

This continued for maybe a minute, or maybe several. couldn't say which. Eventually I opened my eyes to see where I was, surprised to find that I had not moved a single inch off of the attic floor. It was a remarkable puzzle.

I closed my eyes again to see if I could feel it again, but little happened. It was over. I leaned over and picked up another Jar without hesitation, screwed off the cap, and took a very deliberate big gulp of empty Jar air and patiently waited. Nothing. I tried another one. Still nothing. How entirely strange.

Was there something in one of the Jars, but not in another? Or had I simply become accustomed to what was in all of the Jars? Or did that feeling of expanding universe have nothing to do with the Jars whatsoever? I had absolutely no clue at all.

I picked myself off of the floor, this time careful not to hit my head again and glanced across the entire collection of dozens and dozens of Jars and then continued to examine the rest of the attic collection.

Mixed among the stacks of Mason Jars, there was an astonishing selection of Bottles, the kind that you might find at a flea market or antique shop. There were many plain Bottles like soda Bottles, but many of them had a unique shape with few exactly alike. Some were tall, flat and thin, others being squat and round. It was like a collection of glass mushrooms on display in a museum.

Then I saw a mouse and it startled me for a second. I wasn't alone.

The mouse scurried right across the shelf dodging between some Jars and Bottles. "Stingo reincarnated so soon?" It was a possibility perhaps.

Unlike the storage Jars, the Bottles were of a beautiful array of colors, everything from lime green, to cobalt blue, to deep purple, each gorgeously catching the available light from the attic port holes and from my lantern. Most Bottles had some sort of stopper or cork, but a few were even taped shut with electrical tape.

And again, curiously, just like the Jars, each was completely empty with many marked with numbers or even a word. One tiny little blue bottle with a cork stopper was labeled "Cane 14". Another pretty and small triangular green bottle had a piece of tape that just read "31B". On the floor I found a quart Mason jar with a label that read "3.15.61- Stick 42". Next to it a Jar with the name "Henry" scribbled across one side.

An idea occurred to me, "Did it contain jam, a gift for Henry? Or did Henry, whoever that was, make something that was in this Jar once?"

What were these numbers? Why did some have names? And why were they marked "Cane" or "Stick"? Did they once contain varnish for a particular stick? And what did the numbers mean?

This was a puzzle. "Ah," I thought. "Maybe they were presents for people. "Wait- maybe these numbers are dates…"

I soon discovered that everything was arranged chronologically. I went over to one corner, and found the earliest date, and that was on an old red stoppered bottle, fat and round on the bottom with a long tall skinny neck. It said, "10.18.57".

"That's about when Stingo bought the mountain," I conjectured. I then scurried over all the Jars and Bottles, easily a hundred, following the dates until I found the last one on the opposite site of the attic, and it was marked "3.16.63". I double checked and found there were no later Jars than this, and no earlier date than the first one.

I just shook my head. This was something that completely escaped explanation.

Then my attention drew to the Insulators. These looked like inverted glass bulbs, again of a wide variety of colors and shapes. I knew immediately what they were. However, it was doubtful that anyone else stumbling into this attic could so easily identify them. And this was a collection that rivaled many I had encountered. It was beyond belief that Stingo had amassed such a collection, and yet the subject never came up.

Telephone Insulators are those things that everyone has seen high atop telephone poles, but hardly anyone has ever given them a second's worth of thought. They are what are used to connect the telephone line by a twisted wire to the wooden pole crossbeam so that the telephone line doesn't come loose, while at the same time insulating it from being grounded and becoming shorted out in the rain.

When I was a kid about fourteen years old, my ukulele playing buddy Andy introduced me to the bizarre hobby of collecting these Insulators. I quickly became a modest expert on the subject.

Starting in the 1960's you could find Insulators at flea markets and antique shops. Even though Insulators are still being made to this day and fulfill the same function on tens of millions of telephone poles all over the world, the first Insulators are in a category all to themselves.

Currently, Insulators are all made of inexpensive porcelain or rubber and are rarely anything but dirt brown in color. In the late 1800's, Insulators were always glass and came in a wide variety of shades. The best Insulators were known by specific brand usually embossed on the outside of the glass. The reverse side often had the date of manufacture.

I picked up several and immediately recognized the labels: "Hemingray" (also alternatively stamped "H.G", short for Hemingray Glass), "W.F.G." for Western Flint Glass, "Good", and "Surge" stamped on a miniature electrical fence Insulator. There were many others.

The scene of all of these rare Insulators immediately brought back the memory of the extremely obscure N.R. Woodward catalogue that I had bought as a fourteen-year-old through contacts in the Insulator underground. This manual was so rare it wasn't even machine bound, but rather put together by hand one at a time into a three-holed notebook, the kind with the bend down metal fasteners. It was called "The Glass Insulator In America", and was a must have for any Insulator nerd such as myself.

This catalog reproduced hundreds of cross-sectioned diagrams of hundred-year-old Insulators in the same manner in which one might look at medical cross sections of human anatomy. And here in front of me were specimens that I had only dreamed of looking at through Woodward.

Insulators came in green, aqua, sky blue, opaque white, carnival glass orange, deep purple, and other hues. This little collection had a rainbow sampling of them all.

Often, Insulator colors were the result of ultraviolet light striking the chemical constituents inside the glass over years of time up high on the telephone poles. This changed the actual color of the glass which very well may have been perfectly clear upon production. Insulator color was like the aging of wine over many years. For example, purple Insulators became purple as the solar radiation acted upon magnesium present in the originally clear glass. It was magic.

Then my eyes nearly popped out of my socket. I bent down and carefully caressed a small but weighty Insulator that neatly fit into the palm of my hand. It bore only a single star embossed on one side. This was an impossibly rare, red Insulator.

"A Red Star!" I barely uttered in a whisper, "I can't believe it. I thought these were just a myth…"

Red Insulators had been nothing more than a rumor, since no manufacturer had been known to produce that color in any quantity. There was no written record of such a thing in existence, and no one alive had ever actually seen one, including Woodward, who didn't even mention it in his catalog.

There wasn't any practical reason for making a red Insulator besides market branding anyway. It was financially unfeasible- The only reliable method for producing a true red glass Insulator back in the 1800's involved the use of gold particles in the glass itself, and this made production prohibitively expensive. It just wasn't worth all the trouble, and certainly not worth the expense when clear, blue, aqua, and green glass worked perfectly well.

Yet, here I held one in my hand. It was a miracle.

"Son of a gun…" I said to myself. I was tempted to put it in my pocket and run back to my car. I would make the cover of the next edition of "The Glass Insulator In America", except for the fact that I didn't think it was printed any more. But it had been decades since I had concerned myself with these antiques, and I hadn't seen the catalog in ages.

I gingerly put the treasure carefully back in its spot, and surmised I would return when I could properly protect such a fragile object over a rocky trail with padding.

Already the lesson of "Control or "Chance had been burned into my brain.

Then I thought about it for a second.

"Nah!!"

I readily stuffed the little glass Insulator into my baggy trousers pocket.

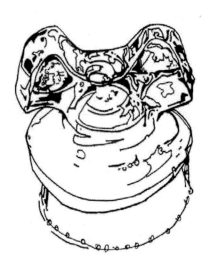

Chapter 17
Paper Baguette

By now my eyes had become quite adjusted to the dim light in the attic, barely lit by the lantern. I was then starting to make out other darker objects in the attic that did not reflect or refract light, but rather were lost in the shadows.

Here and there I found a few cardboard boxes that had a sampling of old brain lab papers, a few more old newspapers, and some of Stingo's old writings and instruction sheets for the lab. No big surprises there.

I looked around some more, and then spotted far in one corner a big rectangular box. I had to crawl over to get to it, as the roof went quite low in that spot.

When I got close I saw that next to it lay a couple of old Brooms and a Fishing Pole. I began to push these out of the way and noted that each had some funny geometric designs on the handle. I didn't think much of it, for the moment.

I soon saw that the box was actually a big luggage chest and that it had a leather strap on the end. I grabbed it and slowly scooted it out towards the center of the attic. It was heavy, so there were things inside it. I couldn't wait to open it up.

It seemed to be an old cargo trunk, the kind people would keep old clothes in.

When I finally had it moved far enough into the center of the attic, I could see that actually resembled a stereotypical treasure chest. It was flat on all sides, but it had a domed top. It wasn't in very good condition. Some kid finding it would probably think that it might have come off an old pirate's ship, although I was fairly certain this wasn't the case. Stingo could certainly be as grouchy as a pirate with a wooden leg, but that was about as far as the similarity went.

I lifted the lid, and it slid off onto the floor before I could catch it. The hinges were broken or gone.

Inside was a potpourri of objects, filling the chest nearly to capacity. For starters there were sticks of all kinds. And by this, I don't mean just plain sticks, but an assortment of stick like objects. This included Canes with bent handles, Walking Sticks with various palm like grips, a couple of old Umbrellas, and a Golf Club. I picked up the Golf Club and immediately thought of my father, a talented amateur who actually won the New Jersey Pro-Am championship one year, the amateur member of the team. My mother still had his silver trophy plate, and I proudly displayed his numerous golf trophies on my own bookshelves at home.

I rummaged through the collection of sticks, and again, I couldn't believe my eyes. I picked up a walking Cane of a design I was intimately familiar with. It was a twin of a rare Cane that I used to play with as a kid that belonged to my grandfather- a Cane that I had never seen anywhere else, ever.

When I was really little, about six years old or so, I used to travel out to my grandparents chicken farm in New Jersey. There my grandfather had a couple of ornately decorated Canes, and I always used to play with them as if they were rifles. Once after my mother took me to see the animated movie *Fantasia*, I was smitten with the segment where Mickey Mouse is the Sorcerers Apprentice. Back then I had pretended that my grandfather's Canes were actually magician's sticks.

Another one of my grandfather's Canes was particularly unique and it looked exactly like a small totem pole, complete with beaked creatures and other figures sitting on top of each other.

But the other was shaped like a regular curved walking Cane, and yet had intricately colored and carved figures on it. This included lizards and snakes as well as flowers, geometric designs and a dragon head. I had never seen another like it before, yet here in the attic, in the most improbable coincidence imaginable, I held its virtual twin in my hands. It looked like it was in absolutely perfect condition, at least as far as I could tell in the dim attic light.

"This is amazing!" I gasped to myself in the wonder of finding another like the original I had at home.

The collection of objects thrown inside this trunk made it seem like an adult's toy chest. Quickly I pulled out more items- an old Typewriter, a neat little box with a beautifully illustrated old Tarot deck inside, and a jewelry box.

I took out the jewelry box and found a couple of little chains inside. One had a little pointed faceted rock, like a piece of blue marble, and the other a little round globe held in a thin clasp of silver. I lifted one and it swung from my hand like a Pendulum. Inside the box were a number of other small marble sized globes of various colors. With a little trial and error I found that each marble could be interchanged within the clasp.

I placed the jewelry box back and rummaged around some more.

Here was a little box of Gibson guitar strings, a tuning fork, and a very primitive guitar capo. Certainly these were items that Stingo had used as a folk singer. I even found a little card that had a list of folk songs on it, numbered one through seven.

"A set list!"

I could only imagine the gig for which Stingo had prepared that list of songs to play. It might have even been for the old Satire Lounge on Colfax in Denver before hardly anyone at all knew his name.

I continued to rummage through the trunk. There were plenty of old celluloid and vinyl records, among them some unidentified discs that I recognized as master pressings made when one manufactures a record album. I could read Stingo's name on them and figured that these were produced long ago when he was first trying to make a name for himself in show business. One of the discs looked like it was a recording for a car commercial, something a disc jockey might put on during a show break. It said "MG Motors".

I looked around thinking there might be something to play the records on, and sure enough, I found it. Inside the chest was a small square box with a hinge and a leather handle. I picked it up, set it on the floor carefully and opened it up. I discovered it was an old wind up portable gramophone.

As a small kid, I momentarily remembered having something similar at the age of five or six. This type of record player didn't have a magnetic needle and a speaker, but instead relied on the mechanical movement of a thick needle in the groove of the record. This vibration was transmitted physically to a two inch diaphragm that was connected adjacent to the needle and reproduced the sound off of the record. The higher frequencies of the sound came immediately right from the diaphragm. The tone arm that held the needle and the diaphragm was hollow inside, and the lower frequencies traveled down this to a chamber and an opening inside the box next to the rotating record platter.

My kid's record player had an electric motor to turn the record platter around, but this one was much older and even that part was mechanical. I searched around inside the player lid and found the wind up handle. I then searched for the place to attach it and wind it up, and found a little silver ringed hole in the front of the case where the handle fit to connect to the spring motor inside.

Within a short time I had wound up the player and flipped the latch that released the platter. Around and around it spun to my delight and amazement.

I went back to the trunk and picked out one of the old celluloid discs and placed it on the record player. It sounded all wrong, and then realized this old player was for old 78 RPM discs, not newer 33 RPM records. I rummaged around, and indeed, found a couple of particularly strange and unexpected old 78's inside. One was a thick "breakable" orange kiddie record made for children.

I placed the needle onto the record and released the motor mechanism. Out came the strains of music certainly made for a five year old. I let the record play on like a strange musical soundtrack to my attic treasure hunting.

The sound of the kid's record up in this strange and spooky space filled with bizarre odds and ends made for a particularly surrealist atmosphere.

I glanced back inside the trunk. I pulled out a typewritten booklet of poems by Stingo. I ignored that for the time. I hate poetry.

There were a few private letters, pieces of fan mail from Stingo's days on his NBC summer replacement show. And then there was a large dog eared manila envelope with a double ringed clasp. This was the kind of envelope that you close by winding a string around each part to keep it shut. It looked like a mouse had sampled the corner it for edibility.

I turned it over and read the scribbled and smeared handwritten label:

BOW WOW
Found, 12– 20–44
Luxembourg

"Wow", I realized. This was from war. But what was inside? Pictures of a people dancing? Jazz Music?

I undid the string and pulled out an old hard bound notebook, like a diary. I brushed my hand across the backside and blew off the dust. I could tell that it was a half-century old; it smelled a like mildew. It was a little bigger than your typical paperback book, although not too terribly thick.

I flipped the notebook over to the front side, and I saw a hand written title inscribed in the center of a decorative oval. "Oh my...," I said as I read the title out loud, barely in a whisper that even the mouse might not have heard what I said.

My heart stopped- I read the title. It said...

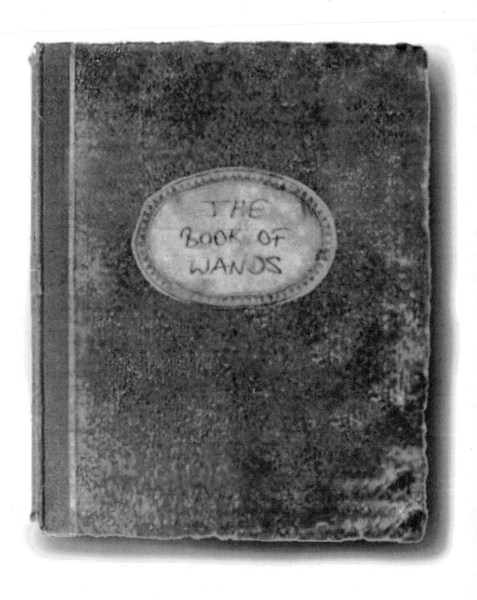

"Wands! Wands!"

It was incredible. That's what the note in the Jar buried at the tree said. I had found it!

Was this one of Stingo's early works? A fantasy treatise on magic? Was it the beginning of story book for kids? Was this a lesson? Was this just one of Stingo's elaborate jokes? I quickly flipped it open looking for his signature. Nothing.

"Wait a second," I thought. I picked up the envelope again and looked back at it-

$$Found, 12- 20-44$$

Knowing Stingo well enough, I knew that he always penned his autograph on every single one of his creations along with a date of creation.

This said "Found".

I quickly looked at the beginning and end of the book, and couldn't find Stingo's signature anywhere, although it was clearly in his own handwriting.

Stingo had told me about being in the Battle of the Bulge numerous times, and this date looked about right. Maybe it was a memento of some sort. I had nothing but guesses.

I began to flip more slowly through the little book. Even in spite of the kerosene lamp I had glowing up there, the dimness of the light inside the attic made reading anything beyond a bold title or chapter difficult, especially as the writing was faded and small. Nevertheless, I tried to read something as best as I could as my curiosity was stronger than my patience to take the book down the ladder and downstairs where the light was a lot brighter.

I came upon chapter headings that made little sense to me, as well as being just about the strangest sounding book chapters I had ever laid my eyes on: "I Am Not A Guy", "Scratching Your Head", "Elephants and Noses", "The Amoeba's Hairpiece", and "A Spinning Layer Cake". This didn't sound

like Wands at all. It certainly didn't sound like Stingo's style of writing which although was weird enough, was so easy to identify as his very own.

This sounded completely different. What *was* this book??

I tried to read the text, but it was too hard to really make out much of anything without generating a good migraine. I could make out a few pictures, and sure enough, I saw simple drawings that looked like sticks, Canes and other things.

I kept flipping through and I could read some more chapter titles that didn't sound quite so weird. I realized these chapters were the same as all of the objects around me in the attic. Umbrellas, Canes, Sticks, Cards, and even a chapter on Jars! "Alright!" I exclaimed excitedly.

This book at least might explain what the heck all these Jars were for.

I couldn't wait to start reading the notebook in detail, but I quickly decided I would first dig around in the trunk some more. I put the book back into the envelope, laid it on the floor, and then started digging through what was left.

There was a big dark piece of cloth. I unfolded it, and realized it was a big flag with embroidered symbols on it.

There were three circles in the middle of the flag, arranged like three cannonballs forming a triangle. The top one was just a circle. The bottom two each had an additional design, one had a dot in the middle, and the other had an X through it. This looked vaguely familiar, and it occurred to me that I had seen something similar on one of Stingo's index cards pinned in one of the cabin walls. I had no idea what these symbols meant, but it must have been important if they made their way onto a big flag.

"Could it have something to do with the brain?" I wondered.

I folded up the flag and set it aside.

Digging around towards the bottom I found another tiny book and pulled it out. This was also very hard to read, and I had to hold it directly close to the lamp to make out anything.

"Oh man!" I exclaimed. It was Stingo's diary from the war! Maybe I could connect the dots and find an entry that would match the date on envelope for *The Book of Wands*.

This was now too intriguing to put off, even if it hurt my eyes trying to make out the writing in the dimness of the lamp light.

I put the lamp down and got down on my stomach right next to the light. I held the diary as close as I could and scurried through all of the pages and dates until I could match the date. I could see that all of Stingo's entries were very brief, often just a few words scribbled down, perhaps to just serve to jog his memory.

Finally I found the exact date and read his entry…

12-20-44

Nightfall, hunkered down in cellar outside some village — waiting for backup, nothing to do but sample found bottles with two pals… Sluuurrppp!

Curiosity among the books: "Livre au Baguettes"— will pocket and translate later with Jacques —

"Wait a minute…Baguette? Isn't that French Bread??"

Now I was really confused.

But that was it. I thumbed through the remainder of the diary, but couldn't find any other references to the mysterious *Book of Wands*.

Perhaps there was something in the book itself. Maybe the book was Stingo's copy or translation of the original.

"Hold on, doesn't *livre* mean 'book' ?" I wondered, a cook book?

I quickly sifted through everything left in the trunk looking for another book. But alas, there were no other books, not an original cookbook or Baguette book in another language.

"Crumb!" I said to myself and the lone little mouse.

Ah well. I was getting a bit tired and my eyes were starting to hurt. I too would save something for later.

I was down to the bottom of the trunk and had emptied it out. I held the lamp inside just to make sure I wasn't missing anything. And it was a good thing I did, because I then noticed something hiding right in the corners- several little sticks, no bigger than Chopsticks.

There were maybe a half dozen sticks in there, along with a Pencil, a couple of old Pens, and even a small Paintbrush.

I picked up one of the sticks. Indeed, it looked like an ordinary Chopstick. But as I held it, I could ever so slightly start to make out a little design that someone had drawn on it, and it looked like a bit of faux basket weaving, a lot of criss-cross hatch marks.

And then suddenly- it was like the clouds opening up on a dark stormy day exposing the sun.

But it wasn't just the sun shining inside my cranium cavity, but a brilliant star flaring behind my eyebrows.

In my mind, a huge star exploded into the entire solar system with flares ten-million miles high. The inside of my head lit up like a cosmic strobe light.

I suddenly remembered something that I had completely forgotten, something utterly blocked from my consciousness for the past five years.

I had suddenly remembered what happened to me years previous, standing at the top of Laughing Coyote Mountain when I had been left all alone at the brain lab for the day, all by myself.

I literally fell back. My mouth just hung open.

How could I have forgotten the details and the events of that day on top of the peak, holding in my hand two Chopsticks exactly like the one I was now holding in my hand inside this dimly lit attic?

It had been a momentous occasion, a stupendous, consciousness rocking experience on top of the mountain. But I had not given it two seconds of thought since the afternoon it occurred- until that very moment.

All these years, I had remembered nothing but a safe screen memory of just another day at the brain lab. I had forgotten the enveloping, inexplicable, frightening vibration that had seemed to come from all around, the sound that sent me scurrying back down to the safety of the forest lower down the mountain.

Now, with this little insignificant looking Chopstick in my fingers, it all came back to me. I was like a person who suddenly in a split second lightning bolt recovers from amnesia and remembers his very name.

I could smell the air on top of the peak from five years back. I could see the brilliant scarlet of the tens of thousands of lady bugs covering the bushes like molten paint. I could hear that utterly incomprehensible sound in my head that seemed to come from everywhere, and yet from nowhere in particular at all.

The sound I remembered was that indescribably subtle, yet ever present electric hum that I picked up like a radio antenna twirling round and round at the top of the mountain, that bizarre noise that eventually rattled me down to my very bones.

The little Chopstick that I held now in my hand was a flashbulb going off and revealing a corner of my mind that had been denied within minutes of the experience long ago.

Most of all- I remembered that FEELING on top of Laughing Coyote Mountain, that FEELING of standing on the edge of another dimension- that FEELING of standing at the edge of INFINITY.

I had a frontal lobes pop at plus 10 intensity, right there sitting on my dirt covered rear end, inside a dusty old cabin attic. It was a Big Brain Bang, as big as any one I had ever imagined.

I glanced down at the innocent little stick in my hand. I knew there was something to this stick that went far beyond its utter plain and ordinary appearance. This wasn't just for scooping up fried rice.

I didn't know exactly what I knew, but I knew a door to a brain bank deposit vault had just been blasted open, and that I was entering another You-niverse. I didn't know where it would lead, but I realized something big in this nuclear mind meltdown.

What I realized was that there are sticks—
and then,

THERE ARE *STICKS.*

BOW WOW 3
Scratching Your Head

Are you confused? Are you disturbing thousands of innocent dust mites that have been comfortably napping on your scalp for the past lifetime?

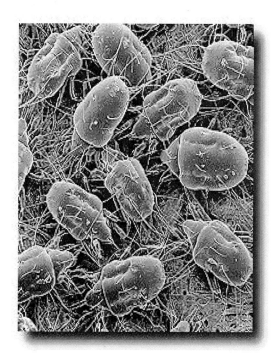

Before, when you have held a book in your hand it probably never occurred to you that there could be somebody HERE.

This is different.

I'm between YOU and this >>> WORD<<<.

Attention! Arf arf arf!!

See the dog?

Look...
Where is THAT dog?

Is it in your brain, or outside your brain or
Somewhere else in between?
To think that the dog is just only in your brain or in
the ordinary world alone would be an egotistical error, a
common misconception that confuses imagination with reality
estate.
I understand that this is a new thing to grasp, to
understand. But I believe you will be a good student, you will
learn. I have faith in you.

Look instead for Me and Fido between the shadow of sleep
and the light of morning.

You are receiving my communications and signals by
method of uncountable trillions of cranial and INTER-cranial
lollipops licking each other, riding on invisible candy roller
coaster cars, on impossibly small neural neutron train tracks.
Ding ding ding ding! Split the atom and watch the bullet cars
of creative thought pass by a million dendrite and axon Train
of Thought track crossings.

Surely by now you are getting the signal.
Someone is looking up, wide eyed, at the traffic signal
blinking green, yellow, red, green, yellow, red, green...
That's you.
Honk, honk! Move it buddy!

It's me making all the noise. I've pushed the big round
button that says, "To cross street, push button."
You see- you must see to Travel- that you are not doing
this solely on your own.

Hold my hand tight, junior. Take a big brave deep breath, step off the curb, plant your feet down, look both ways and cross the street.

There you go.

You're getting it now.

Beep! Beep!

Samuel F.B. Morse invented a code by which nineteenth century settlers could communicate across the wide grass prairie by tapping out short and long bursts of electricity that was carried on long wires strung from pole to pole for hundreds of miles.

People would trade messages with each other by interpreting the electrical clicks that represented letters in the alphabet, that when combined made words that further represented objects or actions.

These people sending these electrical clicks back and forth didn't see each other at all.

Yet, they didn't doubt that there was somebody on the other end.

Soooooooooooh-

You're getting my blip blip blip now.

Me, I'm sending you code.

Ditditdit

Dotdotdotditdit   Dot Dasssssssssssh Dot Dashhhhhhh

ABCDEFG

HIJKLEmmenoP

I am here

Where ever that
is…..

And you, my buddy----

You   are   Waaaaaaaaaaaaaaaaaaaaaaaaaaaaaaaaaaaaaaaaaaay
over

                              Here.

The goal is to Travel from Here to Here, more or less.

A Secret:
I can hear you as well.

I am signaling to you
Come in, YOU

Do you read me?

Alright, Now, it's your turn---
Talk to me.

Tell me something only you know.
                              >>>Now<<<

                              I'm listening

End of Part One